Self-Care to Prepare

B. JUDY

ENVIRON
PRESS

SELF-CARE TO PREPARE

ENVIRON PRESS
TM

To my Parents who showed me
the power of reconciliation and good humor.

To my Brothers
who always have my back and ensure my accountability.

To my extended and chosen family
who showed me the value of intrinsic worth.

To my friends
who provided solidarity and space for transformation.

To my pets
who provide reminders for self care:
food, water, touch, exercise and sleep.

Contents

Dedication   v
Two Notes   ix
Emergency Resources   xi
Endorsements   xiii
Sit and Talk   xiv
The S.T.R.A.W.S. Process   xviii
To Bark, Bite, and Be   xxv
A Welcome to All Readers   xxx
My Un-Apologetic Approach   xxxvii
I Swear to Tell The Truth   xxxix
The W.A.G. Tool   xliii

The Guard at the Gate   1

How Self-Care Helps Us Look Forward   14

Boundaries for Being   22

I am Loved, I am Known   28

Considering Perspectives   34

Integrity, Intent, and Impact   40

Self-Care, Not Self Centered   48

Love > Bias, Burnout, or Bigotry   54

The Social Impact of Self-Care   59

Return to the Heart   63

Notes and References   66

Two Notes

On Content And Trigger Warnings

No More Dogma addresses many sensitive and challenging topics, occasionally with cursing, and many topics from the Bible which you (the reader/listener/recipient) may find disturbing or triggering. The sensitive and challenging content includes but is not limited to: cursing, sexual themes, religious trauma, homophobia, misogyny, sexual assault, rape narratives, slavery, and suicide.

On Footnotes and Literal Thinking

This book includes many footnotes, offered with care and intention. They're here to support readers who appreciate clarity, especially those who—like many autistic folks—may process language more literally. They're also included to gently disarm the kind of rigid, dogmatic interpretations that often rely on hyper-literal readings.

To be clear: I am *not* equating autistic thinking with dogma. One is a natural neurocognitive variation; the other is a belief system that often resists nuance. I honor and affirm neurodivergent ways of understanding—and I believe everyone deserves language that invites understanding, not confusion or harm.

Emergency Resources

Available in the United States

BlackLine - BIPOC & LGBTQ+, call or text
1 800-604-5841 or callblackline.com

LGBTQ National Hotline
1 (888) 843-4564

LGBTQ Immigration and Asylum seekers
immigrationequality.org

The National Coalition of Anti-Violence
avp.org/ncavp/ text or call: (212) 714-1141

National Domestic Violence Hotline
1 (800) 799-SAFE, or text "start" to 88788

Transgender Lifeline with micro grants and a hotline
1 (877) 565-8860

The Trevor Project: support for LGBTQIA+ youth
TheTrevorProject.org

International Emergency Resources

Association for Women's Rights in Development
    AWID.org

Charity Navigator: search for charities
    CharityNavigator.org

Human Rights Watch
    HRW.org

International Lesbian and Gay Association
    ILGA.org

Minority Rights Group International
    MinorityRights.org

Endorsements

As the author of *No More Dogma* I stand within a historical context as both someone who has enjoyed the privilege and the responsibility to serve various communities. I am far from perfect, so as I continue to grow I will continue to explore the ways in which I can use my voice, my vote, and my donations to support diasporic communities. I continue this work today, in part by donating a portion of the revenue from *No More Dogma* to a variety of charities, advocacy groups, and resource centers. My deepest hope is this: if you dream like I do, if you too want to see "No More Dogma" then please take another step toward solidarity together. Please join me in uplifting these organizations, and reach out to these organizations as you have need.

Return to the Heart Foundation: Return2Heart.org

This Indigenous women led organization holds my heart close. These women listen, they follow the lead of matriarchs, redistributing resources where they're most needed: into the hands of Native women and Two-Spirit leaders.

Wesley Theological Seminary: WesleySeminary.edu

Where I learned to listen, to read, to exegete, to wrestle, to question, and to unpack my own dogma, a task I continue to undertake today. Even though I continue to interrogate the claims of faith today, I continue to uplift my seminary. I do not say this lightly: I would not be alive today without my professors and peers in ministry. Continue to draw the circle wide beloved! Would recommend. Would attend again.

Sit and Talk

Imagine that you dear reader have arrived early to an old community center for a support group about how to have difficult conversations. You've been here before and you've enjoyed conversing with everyone. Which is a relief because now at least you know an enough about each person, so the practice conversations during the meeting are a bit easier now. However, that poses a new problem now: you have to once again decide who will sit beside. So you scan the large circle of chairs and see:

1. A former pastor turned atheist with a visible tattoo of bees.
2. A trans woman wearing a red scoop neck tank top and a necklace made of stained glass.
3. A artsy person with paint stains on their shirt and a guitar case at their feet.
4. A former college instructor who likes to bring their favorite pens to these meetings.
5. A two time survivor of rape with CPTSD who noticed you as soon as you walked in.
6. A graduate with a masters degree who was on their e-reader when you walked in.
7. A former conservative, now a leftist, whom you suspect may have some thoughts about gun control.
8. A smiling Scorpio lesbian with keys hanging from a carabiner and sticker covered tumbler at her feet.
9. A previously un-housed person who seems cozy with a cup of coffee and fleece lined plaid sweater.

Now, whom would you sit beside? Note that you have to pick just one conversation partner so you can only pair up with one of these people. Would you say this is a difficult decision? If so, then allow me to make it a bit easier. There is only one person in the room. That one whole person, who saved a seat for you, is me, the author of "No More Dogma." Now why would I, a trans person, split up my various experiences into various identities, especially when trans people are not often treated as a whole person?[1] Well, truth be told, we are all more than the sum of our parts, even those parts that people always want to talk about and define without inviting us into the discussion.[2] When we try to understand a person only based upon parts of their body, parts of their mind, parts of their whole, that approach is wholly inhumane. Subjection is what happens when are made into subjects to be talked about.[3] Absent minded comments are made when we are not fully present and included.

I was raised as a Christian, which means that I would regularly attend gatherings where many people would talk about a being, a God who only joined the conversation in spirit or in old written statements. In that space I was taught how to interpret, how to judge right from wrong, even though most of these sinners were not in the room to be part of the discussion. We had plenty of excuses and reasons as to why these folks didn't attend and we had a whole theology with which to explain why God would not attend, except in spirit. Now to be clear, these spaces don't automatically create dogma, but these kinds of situations are the perfect environment for dogma to emerge. I was glad to have many pastors who would steward these spaces, pruning away any sudden growths in dogma. I looked up to these pastors, and I too wanted to learn how to detect dogma. I too wanted to engage in learning, questioning, admitting what we didn't know, while also defending against any claims to knowing everything just because we claimed to know an all knowing God.

Over time though I would come to see just how difficult and widespread this phenomenon had become. I found that dogma was not limited to any one particular tradition, political view, belief system, culture, scientific institution, or relationship dynamic, even though dogma can emerge in all of these contexts. I kept returning to a hyper focus, a curiosity to spot the difference between those who would nurture knowledge like a living thing versus those who held a death grip on knowledge.[4] I wanted to know how to spot the dogs of dogma, how to recognize their clenched fists before I would get hit again.[5] So I would spend the first two decades of my working career studying these places where dogma would emerge. I befriended many pastors who were worried about people being led astray. I met conservatives who wanted things to be their way and didn't give a shit about someone being gay. I've conversed with hateful christian protesters in the first summer of my transition, and led gatherings about dogma before my own congregation of believers. I've called out my professors for dogma as a post grad student, and mediated discussions in a classroom full of freshmen. So what did I learn about dogma?

All forms of dogma share one strong trait: a rigid, unquestionable obedience to a belief, claim, tradition, or value that defends itself by weaponizing certainty. Sit and stay with that for a moment. Think about how dogma reacts to proposed changes, to challenges to the certainty they cling to with a closed fist. I realized a difficult truth: all of us are capable of being dogmatic. I know that's an uncomfortable thought. However, the root of the problem has been hiding within the root of the word. According to the Oxford Dictionary of Word Origins the root of the word Dogma is *dokien*, which means it *seems good*.[6] Pause here to think about that for awhile. Hold that thought, chew on it a bit, and roll around with it for a bit.[7] Dogma means *it seems*. How ironic is that!? Dogma itself is so rigid, so very sure of itself, so sure of its claims that the dogmatic would risk harming themselves or others over something that *seems to be* true! When we hold something that, at least to us, seems to be absolutely true, we tend to bring that truth out into the world. For awhile it's a walking stick: we learn to lean on it, so if we drop it we of course pick it back up.[8] Then when we can't lean on that stick while speaking with someone who stands on their own without that stick, we are now confronting someone who is unarmed, and we are holding a big stick.

We don't want to go into a conversation where we can't stand up for ourselves: such a situation is ripe for harm and abuse. We also don't want to walk with a stick to confront someone who has brought their own stick: that tends to devolve into violence. So what do we bring to these conversations? We can't beat them, we don't want to join them in spreading dogma, so what can we do to ensure we don't reach our last straw with dogmatic dickheads? We come prepared with a bundle of S.T.R.A.W.S., which is a conversation process, a source of endurance, and an assurance for preserving ourselves in the process.

The S.T.R.A.W.S. Process

So what is the S.T.R.A.W.S. process? The S.T.R.A.W.S. process is a repeatable approach, a plan of lifelong growth away from dogma, a way to reconnect, unite, and hold one another accountable to our responses to dogma.[1] For those who like acronyms like myself you can think of the S.T.R.A.W.S. process as a tool for conversational leverage, helping you have better conversations when you encounter dogma. The S.T.R.A.W.S. process is an outline for "No More Dogma", a repeatable process, and a tool for prying positive outcomes from conversations where dogma emerges. Now I know that is a lot to take in all at once. So before I lose you in the field of tall straws by *telling* you about the S.T.R.A.W.S. process, allow me to *show* you.[2] Imagine with me the setting in which I grew up.

Imagine driving out into the countryside surrounding State College Pennsylvania quite a way, when you come across a tree lined driveway that leads uphill to an acre of grass, surrounded by fields of grain, forests filled with deer, an Appalachian mountain view, and a log cabin.[3] That was my childhood home situated within the ancestral lands of the Susquehannock people, whose relationship with the land stretches back for millennia. My childhood home was surrounded by several apple trees, honey bee hives, and nearby dairy farms. As a descendant of German immigrant farmers I felt quite at home. The matriarch of our family would pass on the values of our family by telling family stories that exemplified hard work, self sufficiency, humor, and distrust toward large government authority exemplified in a long history of volunteerism in mutual aid societies. Which makes sense: our historic belief system is rooted in protest and reformation as protestants. So, despite my protests, I would spend some teenage years doing chores like tending the family garden. Then later paid jobs would include cleaning horse stables on a neighbor's ranch or watering plants at a local greenhouse.

However those summer months would always break with the fall harvest season, which has always been my favorite time of year even though people would do strange things in the fall. Fall was a season for hunters who would pass the time in the woods, making small talk about the dangers of "city folks" while they looked around for something wild to shoot.[4] Fall gatherings would provide a conversation space in which conversations that bonded the family were welcomed, and we could share some dissenting viewpoints, if the matriarch approved. After all, these gatherings were meant to be a time to gather in warmth of making memories with familiar traditions. So our response to Halloween was a mix of cautious suspicion and spirited fun.

For example, during most of the year we tended to dress for comfort, confidence, conversion, coverage, compliance, camouflage, compression, and cultural belonging. Yet during Halloween we use costumes to show others what we find scary, laughable, or sweet. As a trans woman I am often viewed as someone wearing a costume.[5] In their eyes I am either a threat to fear, someone to ridicule, or to belittle, like a child's first attempt to dress themselves.[6] In the eyes of too many I am either a myth to confront, or a bit of fun.[7] I can see it in their eyes as they decide for themselves: is this a trick or a treat? Which means, within a gasp of breath, before I am asked to speak, they decide what I seem to be. Am I a man, a menace, a mess? Do they know my history or do they want to make me history? I am a threat because they don't know what I am concealing underneath. So they approach me. "Oh goody" I think to myself, "another roll of the dice, another stranger approaches with their walking stick in hand."[8]

I grew up here and queer. I know the values that they hold onto: suspicious, self sufficient, and a servant to your community. I understood their misunderstandings, I would endure their name calling before I could claim a name of my own. I was physically quite strong but severely outnumbered. So I would strategize and survive with my voice.[9] Some would give me well meaning advice: punch back, smile more, blend in, hide your tears, find a group of peers, kill them with kindness, pray for them, and stop being you. They wouldn't stop, and I couldn't bring myself to kill myself. So I would cut up my mind, to silence "her", to stop the hurt, and with the scraps I would sew a mask.[10] The process was painful, so I numbed out, and I tried to ignore the painful irony: I was forced to seem to be somebody that I was not. I would ignore the mask I made for the ignorant and over time I would forget myself.

The mask was detached from my being so over time it would decay.[11] As each piece fell away I would develop another conversational tool as I shined through. When I the final piece fell away I could see *her* again. The memory came flooding back with tears of joy: *she* would not be silent. She is the descendant of matriarchy; her inheritance is humor, humility, and hard work. *She* was always within no matter how *it seems*. He just had to get over himself, for he was always the shallow, the mask that would never last. Her voice was always there, always *deeper*, bellowing from the depths to protect the *mask that was he*.[12]

She never needed protection, she knew how to speak, but his coverage did serve a greater purpose. Throughout her life she was growing, her roots were digging deep, and in spring the S.T.R.A.W.S. process emerged, ready to harvest.[13] The S.T.R.A.W.S. process is the result of a lifetime of growth. The S.T.R.A.W.S. process is rooted in the gratitude of past lessons, in the courage to be fully present, and in the hope for a future in which the truth may yet prevail over what *seems* to be true. I am overcome with joy at the thought of sharing my voice with you, but before I do I must acknowledge the other voice which helped me to find my own.[14] So please, allow me to dedicate my work to the memory of a man who dedicated his whole being to every conversation he hosted: my beloved late father, whose initials (B.L.J.) I now carry as my own.

In the early 2000's my dad, being a lovable prankster, got an idea for a Halloween costume: he wanted to be a scarecrow. I suppose he was channeling the spirit of the season. So he assembled a costume with an oversized long sleeve work shirt, blue jean suspenders, work gloves and large boots with straw sticking out of every edge of his outfit. He then sat on a hay bale, tilting his head down so that his straw hat would hide his face, and there he waited by the front door holding a bowl of candy.[15] As each kid approached he would listen well to figure out his approach. When it sounded like a younger kid was approaching he would lift his head with a smile well before the kid and their parent got close so he could welcome them without too big of a scare. For the teenagers though he would let them get close as he stayed quite still before he gave them a good scare. [16]Some would laugh, pointing out how they saw through the illusion and were "for sure" not scared at all. Other teens screamed, and more than one would actually swing their candy bag at him!

I would grow up watching this man do many more pranks and navigate social encounters with a creative charisma. He had this way of approaching every interactions with a transparent intent: to build community and celebrate a connection no matter how much they had in common.[17] He modeled how to listen well for important details, even when he encountered questionable viewpoints. He had this way of surprising people with incredible patience, a sweet demeanor, and quick accountability when he wronged someone. He wasn't perfect, far from it in fact, but as a father he knew who was watching.[18] He was the first person in my life to show me how to turn even a fearful confrontation into an opportunity for deeper connection. He was the first in a long line of conversationalists that I would watch closely as I developed my own approach.

The S.T.R.A.W.S. process was my lifeline, my snorkel when I was drowning in dogma.[19] To be honest, I didn't want this process: I needed it. When I received death threats from strangers, when former friends told me I "deserved" to be assaulted, and when landlords refused to rent to "someone like me" I had to find a way to respond. Turning to the S.T.R.A.W.S. process allowed me to endure the suck of the situation, and a reminder to speak from my roots.[20] Over the years I would continue to hone my craft, buying books along the way, honing my craft with years of public speaking as a pastor, and then through lectures as a college instructor. When she emerged many would try to push my voice to the margins. Little did they know that my voice was already found in the margins of my favorite books, where I took copious notes, and when my voice felt silenced I would recover by listening to the voice of the marginalized, whose voices I hope to uplift throughout.[21]

Beloved, the book you now hold is the process itself.[22] "No More Dogma" is structured into seven chapters, the first outlines what I mean by "dogma" followed by a full chapter for each of then six steps of the S.T.R.A.W.S. process. Each chapter provides the key insights and biblically backed arguments that I use to bash back bigotry. I also strive to accommodate a wide range of readers by reflecting on my diverse range of my experiences. I wrote a warm welcome message to a variety of different readers in the pages ahead, but before we dive in I'd like to give you an overview of the S.T.R.A.W.S. process.[23] Here is a very brief preview of the STRAWS process:

1. Self-Care: preparing for conversations by caring for yourself and others.
2. Transformation: confront, heal, and know yourself before you converse.
3. Reconciliation: conversation strategies for preserving relationships.
4. Accountability: conversation strategies for burning bridges and bigotry.
5. Worth: remembering your innate value after difficult conversations.
6. Solidarity: how better communities and conversations are built together.

I am so excited that you want to strengthen your voice to speak out against dogma. We need your voice! So many of us struggle to even speak up or defend ourselves. So, to you who are willing, who have the opportunity to speak up, I am glad to offer these sharp tools as a way to help you speak up for those who can't.[24] I am just one of the many LGBTQIA+ people who have been misunderstood, objectified, ignored, silenced, bullied, abused, assaulted, or the recipient of death threats as the result of dogma. If this book accomplishes only one thing, then let it be to equip every LGBTQIA+ person and ally with all the tools they need to see no more dogma in our lifetimes. You are part of a diverse movement of like minded people who all want to see the end of dogma.

To Bark, Bite, and Be

Now that we've been introduced to the S.T.R.A.W.S. process as a tool, lets now talk about how we can use this tool, and then we will say hello to some of the folks reading along with us. After all, the S.T.R.A.W.S. process is just a tool, like a crowbar, is a way to personalize your conversations by leveraging your experiences, context, and identity.[1] Which means the S.T.R.A.W.S. process is also an invitation to rethink who you are and how that version of you would handle dogma[2]. For example, do you *recognize* yourself as a fixed being, or do your experiences *reveal* the ongoing story of you? Are you progressing forward by experiencing life? How are you the result of experiences, those vivid memories where, in the silence of your undivided attention, did you witness your becoming?[3] If you are beginning to answer these questions with stories from your life, then you are engaging in a process that Dan McAdams, Ruthellen Josselson, and Amia Lieblich characterize as "a conversation of narrators, or perhaps a war of historians in your head."[4]

Which means that inside your mind, you often tell yourself different stories about who you are. Sometimes these stories may even disagree with each other. You therefore know some of the risks and rewards already; you've been here before many times. Conversations with conflict are not a bug, they are a feature, they are a part of what it means to be human.[5] The stories of overcoming conflict are the stories of humans being, of overcoming, not to spite being, but to be defined, to be understood, heard, loved, for all our being. So when I call for the end of dogma I am not against conflict. Rather, I am calling for trust and support between people that is built slowly through mutual respect and honest conversations. I am proposing a process that ends dogma with an earned, respectful solidarity. Where we move through the process solid, whole, bringing our *full being* through conflict, where change coexists with conversations, but without conflation or coercion.[6] I know that's confusing for many but you're not alone. So let me reflect on a space where many of us have been so we can imagine these dynamics.

As a former college educator and pastor I would lead conversations by following the humility exemplified to me by bell hooks, who would intentionally author her works with a lower case name to elevate the exchange of ideas as more important to her than her title, and to uplift the memory of her great grandmother.[7] In her book *Teaching to Transgress* I would learn to distinguish the difference between those who speak to empower others from those whose who would speak "to silence" others.[8] These words would reframe how I understood conversation dynamics. These words would even reform my own beliefs. I would rethink the presumed silence of the christian God.[9] I would begin to see how "grace" could weaponize silence, where Christians would not act on their beliefs, instead choosing to postpone justice until a day of judgment, which gave power to the voice of wrong doing in the interim.[10] I became more proactive, seeking out silent and silenced voices.[11] My career would accelerate this search as I was employed to seek out, to hear from those whom I have not heard from in awhile. Whether that was visiting shut in congregants, calling on the quiet kid in class, or questioning a curriculum that would not "name the Native nations that have lived on this land for millennia."[12]

Then I listened to the feedback: people don't like being called on, called out, nor called into a victim role for a savior narrative.[13] So I would listen more: I wanted to contribute to the group project of humanity.[14] Yes, group projects, remember those? These group projects were despised by so many of my students for the same reason: not everyone holds themselves accountable to their portion of the work. As I researched this resistance I would come across Dr. Paulo Freire who characterized the challenge of the human project as the need for human action, where each person must transcend themselves, to overcome their own limited selves[15]. In other words: we have to get over ourselves.[16] Our conversations are connected to our identity, to who we imagine ourselves to be. When we speak we acknowledge the importance of listening, of being heard and understood. These are intentions, goals for speaking. So what is our goal? Do we speak to demand respect? Do we respect the power of those who speak? When we listen, if we listen, do we see evidence of the speakers awareness; are they aware of the enormous responsibility they hold with their voice?

Furthermore, do we accept accountability over what we say, how we listen, and what it means to stay silent? These are complex questions. We can begin to answer these questions by looking at the consequences of our conversations. For example, Dr. Tyson Yunkaporta speaks about the accountability behind communication is rooted in the exchange, a kind of transfer of "living knowledge" where our energy and resources are not just stored within an individual.[17] Which means that when people have conversations, they share valuable ideas and understanding, not just facts. I've preached about a similar point before, like when I discussed how Jesus stopped a crowd from stoning a woman accused of adultery.

I would speak about how Jesus, while in the middle of teaching at the temple, would be confronted by the dogmatic of Jesus day. They wanted him to use his power, his voice to support the subjection of this woman's life and body: to kill her because she had sex outside of marriage (John 8:1-5). Jesus knew the real issue: these men wanted a scapegoat, they wanted to avoid accountability. Jesus refuses to be complicit, so rather than respond, Jesus kneels down to write in the sand, listening to see whether anyone would speak up to defend this woman.[18] Then after some reflection he stood up to speak up for her. He pointed out their hypocrisy: they did not take time to reflect, to empathize with her, to think about what they may have in common with others before they speak, and then he returned to being an example by kneeling down again to resume writing in the sand (John 8:6-8).

You probably know the rest of the story: those hypocritical historically horny older men would walk away first, followed by the young pups, leaving just Jesus, the second generation virgin, alone with this sexually active woman. (John 8:9). In that conversation space Jesus encourages her to speak, asking a simple question, and then we can finally resolve this conflict once we hear her speak: nobody has judged my choices, not even this virgin (John 8:10-11). When I gave these sermons in the past I would take the opportunity to uplift these issues as a present danger: judgment is easy, so we too often externalize the work of good judgment that was meant to face inward. So, often without even realizing what we are doing, we pick our walking stick, we speak while ignorant to the voice, identity, history, and inherent worth of the whole being that stands before us. So please, as I draw closer to welcoming our fellow readers, please first listen to Dr. Leanne Betasamosake Simpson, who spoke about the violence facing indigenous women when she said "we have to be careful that our protocols and teachings remain alive in the context of relationships of love, trust, respect, and agency, and that they are not reduced to rules and dogma."[19]

Over the years I would approach the pulpit, feeling the weight of this enormous responsibility, aware of the power of this position, having spent the previous week enjoying the privilege of studying under the wonderful tutelage of the professors from Wesley Theological Seminary in Washington D.C.. So when I arrived at the alter each week I knew I had to contextualize the text, to read beyond one book, all to ensure that I did not risk propagating dogma. I had to make a choice. Would I call upon my congregants to care for others as much as they cared for themselves? Or would I re-crucify Christ, condemning him to consumption, to crumbs and a chrome cup?[20] I knew I did not need to solve the tension; as a leader, my role was to stand in that tension. That tension is rooted in our ability to discern and dialogue even with our differences. In our conversations we need to know whether our differences make us diverse, divided, or distinguished.

A Welcome to All Readers

With that in mind let's say hello to the the diverse groups of people, many of whom are already doing the work that helps us stand and speak together. Let's go in alphabetical order here and say hello!

To my Atheist readers: As a former pastor and former believer I carry the hurt of religious trauma with me. So no, I won't be trying to convert you back to the faith. Granted, *No More Dogma* does quote extensively from the Bible, but that is not meant to treat the Bible as a primary source.[1] Rather the Bible is centered in this conversation for a different reason. You have probably experienced a dogmatic believer whose commitments to the text form a circular logic where they claim a belief, and then provide "evidence" for that belief by quoting from the same source being scrutinized, which is the Bible. I am aware of that logical fallacy.

However, many of the atheists and former dogmatic believers have found their knowledge of the Bible to be helpful to their counters to dogmatic beliefs. Anecdotally I have watched how atheistic and agnostic arguments could be strengthened by knowing the Bible. That observation informed the creation of this book. So what follows is critical thinking applied to biblical knowledge to develop an interfaith argument and process to systematically dismantle dogma at its source, with its favorite source. Though I am of course counting on every reader to bring their own experiences, outside resources, and skepticism.

Christian ally readers. First, please know that you are opening a text that is critical of the over reliance over the *literal* interpretation of scripture.

Also, please know that taking scripture literally is not always bad, but as you probably know, some of the most dogmatic of believers tend to overemphasize a literal reading of scripture. Such an approach can create some rather horrific and harmful readings of the text. I address some of these sections with a harsh comedic criticism that some Christians may find offensive, especially those within the fourth chapter covering accountability.

So please keep these three things in mind as you read. First, thank you so much for being here, for refusing to be complicit in dogma. I know you've faced pushback, even from fellow believers. So again, thank you for persisting. Second, please take care of yourself. "No More Dogma" begins with self-care for a reason: burnt out allies may serve as a testament to the work they have done, and a condemnation of every other believer who has not stepped up to do the work as well. However, burnout can lead to a refusal to engage further. Jesus is already your savior and martyr. I love that for you and I know you do too.

Finally, please remain connected to your communities of faith as you read. *No More Dogma* will often provide a parody of dogmatic beliefs by taking a literal reading of the text to an extreme. The Bible is already a challenging text for apologetics, and the satire within is unapologetic. So please, read with caution, an open mind, and expect some challenges along the way. I normally would not explain a joke but I will here. My satirical take of the text is meant to highlight three major issues within dogmatic beliefs: a refusal to read the Bible, a tendency to put ones own bias into the reading, and the tendency to assume understanding without good exegesis. So please, whenever you feel challenged by a section of this book, please exegete the passages I am referencing. Good exegesis can include:

· Re-reading passages across various translations.
· Reading the whole chapter surrounding the passage.

- Studying the original Hebrew, Aramaic, and Greek translations.
- Seek out a good bible commentary for your particular belief system.
- Divide the work and study the text in groups.

Think of this as a low stakes form of practice. When you sharpen these skills you will start to see who has studied well before making claims. Let these insights (or lack of) be prompts in your conversations. I won't always tell you when I'm being dogmatic myself, and that is the point. I do this on purpose. Faithfulness means being ready to call out the misuse of the Bible. Remember what Paul said: our scripture is to be used for teaching, criticism, skill development, and prepared to do good work (2 Timothy 3:16-17). Wait, pause. Did you actually look up that verse? Come on, we just talked about this love. We need to do better at calling out the misreading, misuse, and abuse of the text before it turns into dogmatic worldviews; that is how we got into this mess. Keep the good faith, study well, and show that good work future conversations.

To my **Comedy loving readers**. Take a look around at this list! Do you see it? I'm sure some of you are imagining the setup to some jokes already. Me too. However, I want to be quite clear: humor is a great tool when you're not a tool.[2] Our jokes need to punch up, to punch out to, but never punch down upon those with less power.[3] Writing jokes about marginalized groups is for lazy hacks who want to *seem to be* funny. Be better; do better. Callout dogmatic dickheads. We don't do better just for the sake of the craft, but for the sake of all those marginalized people who are most deserving of that sense of relief we feel when our voice releases the tension, freeing all of us to laugh along. Do you want a good example, or at least an example of an attempt? Keep reading.

To my **Dogmatic readers**. Well, this is awkward. Are you lost? Maybe that's not a fair question. After all, we can all fall into dogma on occasion. So feel free to keep reading; I can't and wouldn't stop you. Although, while I have you here could you please consider two things and then answer a question for me? First, I want you to know that I was once quite dogmatic, but I've been working on that for some time now. Second, my harshest criticisms are callouts against dogma, so it may get a bit uncomfortable for you.

So before you proceed I'd like to ask you about your comfort. In particular, how do you sleep at night? Do you ever need melatonin, or are you plenty comfortable with ignorance? Do you avoid public transit because you got tired of everyone asking you "where do you get off?"[4] If so, then why are you so obsessed about where everyone else likes to get off? Though, all jokes aside, I really am glad you are here, whether you were gifted a copy of *No More Dogma* or purchased a copy for yourself. Just know, you should keep reading too.

To my Islamic readers. Hello! First, allow me to say that I honor your courage, your questioning, and your sacred fire as fellow critics of dogma in your own right. I admit that I still have much to learn about the Islamic faith. However, I have no doubt that you know more than enough about your own faith and the Holy Qur'an to begin to speak out against dogma. However, please know that I am here for you too. The S.T.R.A.W.S. process is designed to help you speak up as well. Whether that is speaking up about the centuries of crusaders, colonizers, or to any clueless coworkers who weaponize their dogma against you. Please know that I see you, and *No More Dogma* stands with you against Islamophobia. As-salaamu 'alaykum.

To my Jewish readers. Shalom! I'm sure you may be wondering whether you are welcome, so please allow me to be quite clear by saying more than shalom to you all. First, please know that "No More Dogma" affirms our mutual willingness to wrestle with words, and to stand against any violence perpetuated by dogma. Also, yes, I see the irony of my S.T.R.A.W.S. process. I'm sure even your children are more familiar with Vayikra than the average christian, and ignorance like this could be weaponized to spread even more dogma. However, these dangers are part of my reasoning for moving *toward* the Shemot. The intended affect is to first foster an appreciation for an ongoing process, one that emphasizes repetition, where we can recognize our process of becoming someone who examines their own unfolding narrative, and then re-imagines their role within the larger community. These steps are meant to prepare each reader toward a more thoughtful approach, and a mutual commitment against dogma.

To my LGBTQIA+ readers. Hello family, how are you doing? I know you're next to last in this alphabetical list, but please know you have remained in my heart even before I began the first draft. I know you may not trust me yet, you're probably not alone there. Even so, I look forward to earning and honoring your trust, should you choose to extend it. Please know that you are more than enough as you are now. You are loved. You belong. My pronouns are she/her or that bitch over there. You can usually find me nose deep in the spine of a good book (look at that reference section) and sipping from my purple tumbler.

While we are on the subject of people spotting me in the wild, can I ask your opinion on something? Do you ever grow tired of being called "brave" or "courageous" for being you? Personally, I know it's meant to be a compliment, but we shouldn't *have to be* brave. If inclusion, acceptance, and love did lead the hearts of others then we wouldn't need to be brave to be out as ourselves, agreed? If I do have the pleasure of meeting you in person some day (and I hope I do) then tell me what you think. Until then, Love ya!

To my Privileged readers. If by now you are not sure where you fit on this list, then just know, you belong here. You probably assumed as much already, but I will say it anyway: yes, we need your voice too! I would offer you a gold star but that's not something that we lesbians give out anymore. Hang in there though, your privilege is a power we need in the fight against dogma.

Now, I just wrote a welcome to each of the possible readers. I identified who those messages are intended for, but I'm quite certain that many of us were curious. Some of you probably read through each welcome to see what I would say to each group (I know I would). If you did abstain then please, don't. Feel free to go back and take a peek! You can glance at these messages which were intended for others. I say this because I trust most of you have good intentions. I am assuming you won't try to interfere with their delivery, nor misinterpret their meaning by assuming they were all meant for you. Granted, these personal notes were all collected under one book so I can understand if you thought they were all for you, and to some extent they could be.

Although, what if you didn't have that intention clearly laid out? What if I collected these welcome statements and put them into a different context? Just imagine, gathering these letters together, each written to a different audience, then pass these words ahead in time several thousand years to a time when the English language looks quite different. They would have to be interpreted into a modern language, distributed into a different context, and to a different audience without any explanation! Imagine what you would be thinking as you read.

My Un-Apologetic Approach

The Bible is a canon, a collection of letters, poems, laws, visions of an apocalypse, prophecies, song lyrics, narratives, wisdom sayings, and more. Over several thousand years, across numerous cultures and languages this collection of texts underwent many transformations: books were cut, others were added, collected together, translated, edited, revised and debated. The resulting collection can be quite confusing. Some readers come with good intentions, yet their confusion builds. Perhaps they wanted to become a better person, but reading the Bible felt like moving into a new apartment, then reading through the previous owners mail.[1] Some of us put it aside as it doesn't seem to be addressing them, others make copies to pass around so they can read together in groups, and some argue that we shouldn't be reading that mail anyway. Some though see an opportunity. They recognize how they can use these sources for personal gain and avoid accountability for any accusations of harm. They uplift the Bible to hide the ways they are abusing people.

This is why the Bible is the most cited resource in *No More Dogma:* to help you develop the ability to recognize these patterns. One of the most common strategies of the dogmatic is to bring up verses that seem to support their views when taken literally, out of context.[2] My favorite response to these attempts is to parry with parody. Keep this in mind as you read *No More Dogma*: my apologetics are unapologetic criticisms. Again, I'm not against the Christian faith in any way. What I am against is bad faith actors and abusors who try to hide behind a manipulative reading of the Bible. Think of dogma as a twisted vine that has wrapped around the Christian faith. So please pace yourself, think critically, and do good exegetical work.

Now, I will continue to show you how to do both in the chapters ahead and I have already introduced the basics of exegesis. I'm sure many readers are already familiar with critical thinking, but here are the basics. Critical thinking means:

- Look for logic: who or what works together well?
- Look for differences: how many points of view support the claim?
- Look for bias: whose beliefs, or context have more influence?
- Look for inequity: who benefits more from the ideas being presented?
- Look for humility: whose skills or success do you notice the most?

Without these tools working together dogma can find support for sexism, slavery, genocide, and ableism within the Bible. To avoid these same issues I provide a variety of citations throughout to both reveal some broader themes within the Bible, and to help you speak out against these abuses. I will also direct you to numerous other authors, experts, and thought leaders, each of which I recommend to you for further reading. All of these points are woven together with various arguments, tips, and tools that I have organized into a book length explanation of the S.T.R.A.W.S. process. Before you begin reading though I want to answer one of my most common questions and then give you the most important conversational tool.

I Swear to Tell The Truth

I expect you may have one big question for me: will I keep swearing, and if so, why? Yes, but also no. I don't curse just to be edgy. Nor do I support cursing for power and domination. Examples of these include slurs against a race, gender, or sexual orientation. I also don't support intimidation nor escalation of conflicts through cursing. Some people curse out of habit. Others use it as a way to release their emotions. However, I curse for several reasons that are rooted in my experiences. First, I use curse words to emphasize how and why curse words will come up in a conversation. So when I do curse here I am showing you rather than telling you, giving you the experience of cursing in conversations.

Second, I swear to emphasize how cursing is a sleight of hand trick, like a magician performing a miracle, I curse to try to push you toward or away from a thought. However, unlike a magicians show or a conversation with the dogmatic, my cursing is written down.[1] Which means you can, and should, re-examine the context in which one hears a curse. For example, you can understand why I may shout "fuck" as I swerve to miss a head on collision with someone who fell asleep at the wheel. I swear here to However, when we hear swearing in a conversation we often assume the curse make a strong point, start a fight, or create strong feelings. All of these things can be true, but I don't ever intend to use curse word here just to start a fight. Rather, I curse to either emphasize a point or to help you get some emotional distance from a harmful idea.

However, some of the most important information sits just before we curse. Let's say that you arrived to the scene of my car crash an hour later. You didn't see it happen. However, you are late for work so you aren't feeling empathetic when you finally get through the traffic jam to see me there with my demolished car. So you roll down your window to shout "you can't park your car in the middle of the road!" I'm already in shock, I'm injured, my friends are all in shock, and my buddy in the back seat was was rushed to the hospital. So when you roll up, ignorant of the context, unaware of the hurt I'm carrying, without a thought spared for my loved ones who not see tomorrow, then yeah, I'm gonna shout "fuck you".

When we comment or judge without context, compassion, or critical thinking we create the conditions in which dogma and conflict emerge. Both of these are offensive, but dogma is always harmful. Cursing is far less harmful when we curse out the powerful, but far more harmful when the powerful curse those with less power. For example, I've seen mothers hold some shock when they hear their child say their first curse word. However, would you agree that a parent cursing out their child is far more harmful? That is the difference in power dynamics. I've worked blue collar jobs where I heard swearing all day, and I've seen reporters give public apologies for saying shit during a live broadcast. I've also had people confront me to tell me that they were offended by my mere existence, as if I am a living curse. That is not a misunderstanding, that is someone trying to exert their power and trying to control me.

I will continue to unpack the power of language and how these attempts to control language have done actual harm. For now though I think you see my point. I am both a witness, and a victim, of numerous such harmful experiences. I carry the hurt of so many marginalized and LGBTQIA+ peers, some of whom are no longer with us. So yes, I will swear. I swear to emphasize. I swear to provide context. I swear to provide an argument to help push back against any further harm brought by ignorance and dogma. And I swear to push in, to cleave open and create a space in which the voices of previously silenced individuals may be found. So please, either bear with me toward solidarity while I swear a bit, or please, fuck off. Otherwise, we can team up for the dog days of dogma, right after I introduce our more important tool: the W.A.G. tool.

The W.A.G. Tool

You've likely already encountered a kind of W.A.G. tool before. Think of the W.A.G. tool as a cheat sheet, except our conversations are an open book test. Yes, a S.T.R.A.W.S. based conversation will test you, but it's an open book test so you can W.A.G. your way through. I'm sure some of you are more excited than others now. I admit my bias: I am among the girlies, gays, and theys who like a good spread of sheets.[1] I know others will be moaning about yet another hack or tool. However, here are three important considerations. First, I hear you, and no, you don't have to whip out their W.A.G. tool to prove your good nature to every barking bigot. Most folks don't expect such a structured approach to something as organic as a conversation so bringing out the W.A.G. tool can bring up a bunch of reactions. I have had some people walk away, others have more respect when they see how much the subject means to me, while some want to look at the tool and have a conversation structured around the tool itself.

However, the structure behind the W.A.G. tool can help more difficult conversations flow better. Which brings up a second consideration: I am formatting a W.A.G. tool for you to use which you will be able to access after the second book of the series comes out. So you don't need to worry about making a W.A.G. tool of your own. What you do need to consider though is what I believe to be the most important reason for using the W.A.G. tool: it's an accommodation. If you can bring a W.A.G. to a conversation then you are accomplishing a bunch of goals all at once:

- It begins with a safety plan for responding or walking away.
- Your values and rights are presented at the start.
- Its a reference for your intentions, topics, and references.
- It's a blank canvas for creative types to draw conclusions.
- It helps neurodivergent peers (like me) remember.
- It helps you stay on point and stick the landing.
- Deaf and hard of hearing peers will appreciate it too.
- Others will see that you prepared: that demands respect.
- You can exchange them ahead of time if it helps.
- It shortens the conversation for fatigue based disabilities.
- A paper trail enables accountability and justice.
- It allows you to practice before and remember after.
- The topics are now "out in the open" to address together.
- Some respond better to evidence based conversations.
- Text-to-speech and translator apps need it anyway.
- It boosts your confidence, and reinforces your boundaries.
- Others can follow your reasoning when it's structured.

And now, my favorite reason for using the W.A.G. tool: have you ever met a dog who greets you with their whole body? You've probably seen the same dog, with the same body, use their whole being to switch between best friend mode and growling defender. Yet it's the same dog bringing their whole being into every interaction. The W.A.G. tool is structured to remind you to bring your whole being.[2] The front end reminds you of your worth. That beginning has a nose to sniff around first, then a mouth where you can smile, bite, or bark "leave me be!"[3] This has the quick reference safety check, a checklist of self-care affirmations, including a list of rights.

The middle section is a flexible spine, where the heart of your being holds the *answers*.[4] This space helps you remember your goals, your points, your quips, comebacks, and references for any research you may have done. I've seen this section written out, filled with fun doodles, written out as a fiction story to help remember, and even song lyrics. This section helps you to remember your whole being even when you're caught in the middle of a challenging discussion. Then the tail end is a place to *grow*. Here is where you take notes during the conversation to help you remember what was said and to help you reflect after the conversation is over. This last section is an evaluative tool, helping you stay present as you process, deciding when to move on and whether you should W.A.G. with them again. Speaking of which, let's move on to some self-care.

A Few Quotes to Consider

"Like one who grabs a dog's ears is one who passes by
and meddles in a quarrel not his own"
- Proverbs 26:17, World English Bible

"You shall be holy men to me, therefore you shall not eat
any meat that is torn by animals in the field.
You shall cast it to the dogs."
- Exodus 22:31, World English Bible

"Outside are the dogs, the sorcerers, the sexually immoral,
the murderers, the idolaters, and everyone
who loves and practices falsehood."
- Revelation 22:15, World English Bible

"Looking forward, I see evidence of a conflict
more severe than any yet fought by reformation or science;
a conflict that will shake the foundations of religious belief,
tear into fragments and scatter to the winds the old dogmas
upon which all forms of Christianity are based."[1]
- Matilda Joslyn Gage, 1893

Chapter 1

The Guard at the Gate

Have you ever been bent backward by Bible bashers barking bigotry?[2] Me too. What you have experienced is dogma: the canines of convictions who cannot consider critique.[3] Can these old dogs be taught new tricks?[4] Sure! Can we bring some bacon treats to see if they sit, stay, and listen?[5] In theory, absolutely, but in practice it often feels like adopting a stray before understanding their needs.[6] Good intentions without careful preparation is like approaching a snarling stray with bacon and a leash. We hope kindness will be more contagious than whatever they could transmit.[7] We want to believe that they could change. That if we could just show up with truth and tenderness, then maybe they would stop barking. Yet without grounding what we care about within ourselves, our bacon is brushed aside and brunch becomes a brawl.[8]

How do we reach out to loved ones and dogmatic dickheads? To answer that question requires both a thorough understanding of the problem, and a process to guide our approach. Part of our challenge is in misunderstanding why the dogmatic react to our conversations like a cornered stray.[9] What we need is both a better approach, and something better to offer when we can get close. Now I have already introduced the S.T.R.A.W.S. process, which are a set of conversational tools, and biblically backed responses to dogma to help you bash back bigotry.[10] However, even the best tools and arguments are ineffective when we can't identify which caustic convictions to carve out.[11] Within that restrictive space, our conversations feel like leading someone by pulling at their fish nets.[12] I've been there—gently tugging on what seemed like one frayed thread in someone's views, but then I poke a hole, I cut a thread, I begin to unravel their entire worldview by accident.[13] I understand their anger, I worry about ripped fishnets too.

What I meant as an invitation to curiosity was too often received as a betrayal.[14] Suddenly, I wasn't asking questions—in their mind they thought I wanted to expose them. My intentions were misunderstood so let me be clear now: when I say there is a better way to pull this off I don't mean literally. What I mean is the S.T.R.A.W.S. process, which is a better, more thoughtful way to show up in an interconnected world. Thus, the arguments presented within will be woven together as well to help you better address the interconnected arguments of dogma.[15] With these tools we can decide upon a spectrum of goals. For some our goal can be to reconcile the dogmatic back to a willingness to learn about and accept those who are different from themselves. While on the other end, an accountability conversation provides the tools for putting down the dogmatic rhetoric against LGBTQIA+ people.[16]

So let's take some time now to give an example conversation to highlight some of the many of arguments for dogma and their counter arguments which we will unpack throughout the *No More Dogma* series. Let's imagine this through a fictional conversation. Imagine the Garden of Eden as our setting, which hosts a tree whose fruit offers some killer knowledge about right and wrong, if you choose to partake (Genesis 2:16-17).[17] Our conversationalists will be Adam and Eve. Eve likes to be informed, so when she received a contradictory second opinion about the tree she decides to investigate (Genesis 3:1-4). So she approaches the tree, wanting to know what God intended to keep from her.

Once she found the fruitful tree to see what knowledge was being withheld she had her answer: it offers wisdom, a form of knowledge about good and evil. Having that kind of knowledge could help Eve grow in self knowledge, self sustainment, critical thinking, increased empathy, a sense of justice, improved relationships, emotional regulation, responsibility, a greater sense of purpose and more. So she takes a bite, and upon realizing the benefits of knowledge she offers it to Adam. Except, Adam refuses at first. Adam doesn't want to grow to be self aware, knowledgeable, empathetic, or responsible. Adam seems to be quite dogmatic about his choice, so Eve speaks first.

"Oh come on Adam, it wouldn't kill you to change your mind. I mean look at me: I took a bite and I'm fine!"

"I'm not hungry" Adam grumbles as he starts to walk away.

Eve can feel her jaw clenching, but she holds back what she wanted to say because she knows better now.[18] "Well, what if I make it into a drink?"

Adam shrugs and turns to lean against a tree.[19] He spots some wheat blowing in the breeze beside him, so he swipes a fistful of wheat.[20] He drops all but one stalk of wheat which he sticks in his mouth to suck on. Eve knows that look, so with a light sigh she strides over to a nearby pile of dried reeds.[21] After looking it over she finds a reed with a nice dry section of growth between nodes. She picks it up knowing that section of reed will be hollow in the middle. She snaps off a section of growth between the nodes to make a straw. She then jams the straw into the fruit and walks over to Adam, offering it to him. Without looking at her Adam sighs "I'm not thirsty either."

Eve feels her shoulders tighten.[22] She knows this feeling too, but Adam doesn't know. How could he know? "Adam, could you just try it please? You don't know how much this means to me!"[23]

Adam rolls his eyes over to meet her gaze,[24] "I liked you better when you didn't talk so much." Eve's toes curl, calfs tighten, and chest burns as she squeezes the soft ripe fruit.[25]

"Are you serious" she says as she shakes the fruit at him.[26] "Look, I've eaten and I know I feel better. God said I would die—but I am not dead.[27] I wasn't sure at first either but I know better now—"[28]

Adam pushes off from the tree, then turning to face Eve he glares as he closes the distance to her[29] "What do you mean you know better?!" Adam yells "You mean you haven't died yet—well who cares. God said you *will* die. Do you think you can change God's perfect creation?" Adam's suckled wheat shoot falls from his lips to the ground, so he wipes his mouth with the back of his hand while he stares down at Eve. Eve lowers the fruit, but she doesn't move. Eve looks away to see a fawn fleeing between the trees, which are now rustling as a flock of great tits take flight.[30] Eve's chest begins to burn with righteous indignation.[31] Eve thinks to herself "Why does he think so little of hanging out? What exactly is his future plan, to just work for his father?" Eve glares at Adam; she has her answer.[32]

*****

Now, I'm thrilled to continue the story here, as I'm equally excited to witness the ongoing dialogue. Yes, I acknowledge that I've raised a series of theological and ethical questions. After all, Eve's desire for Adam to accept the responsibility of knowing good and evil is a central theme. I'll promise to explore these thoughts more in our fourth book, which will focus on accountability in great detail. However, I don't want you to miss the important dogmatic arguments and counterarguments that form the S.T.R.A.W.S. process. The exchange you're about to witness serves as an example of the arguments that will be explored during the preparation phase, which are a combination of the first two steps of the S.T.R.A.W.S. process. The whole process is interconnected, where each section supports the rest, but you will see this as we continue. All you need to remember for now are the three distinct sections of the S.T.R.A.W.S. process. I struggle with my memory so I like to use another acronym here: P.R.Y. which means:

1. **Prepared** with Self-care and Transformation: these first two are all about how to anticipate and remain ready for a conversation.

2. **Resources** for a Reconciling or Accountability conversation: the second two form a spectrum of conversational approaches, tools, and arguments.

3. The **Yield** of Self Worth and Solidarity: how to recover, stay connected, and create community by repeating the process.

So, with these considerations in mind, we will now imagine that Adam and Eve are in our present day. As they journey through the wormhole toward our present day, Adam grabs the apple and takes a bite.[33] They both arrive in our century, where they have the opportunity to grow up more and develop in our modern context. Today, they both possess accumulated knowledge, wisdom, and experience. However, when we reunite them, we realize that they still hold differing viewpoints. Adam will argue in favor of dogma. Eve is prepared: she has counterarguments informed by self-care and transformation so she is ready to clarify her concerns with dogma. Let's now return to their conversation. We will commence with Eve responding to Adam's final point. Are you ready? Let's proceed!

*****

Adam sits at one end of a conference table in a rolling chair, and Eve is at the other end. Both have their W.A.G. notes before them. Eve is clothed in both knowledge and a comfy three piece suit—with pockets![34] Adam is wearing a similar three piece suit, but his sleeves are rolled up. Adam looks ready for a conversation, so Eve begins.

"Adam, the last time we spoke you were discussing what God said in the garden. Let me know if I understood your point correctly. I believe you were appealing to God's fixed nature, where what God says cannot be questioned. Are you saying that in a world of constant change and conflicting opinions, dogma provides a solid foundation for knowledge? Which would mean that dogma offers a sense of stability and certainty by anchoring belief systems in something fixed.[35] Do I have that right?"

"Essentially, yes."

"Okay. Well, I worry that dogma would discourage inquiry. This interpretation of questions as disloyal can hinder people from refining or deepening their understanding though."

"Eve, that sounds like an appeal to a deeply personal issue. Various traditions address issues like these by pointing to truths revealed by God, which are therefore beyond human revision."

"Adam, that is an appeal to authority. I can appreciate the diversity of belief systems that have emerged even as the Biblical canon was changed and re-translated many times. However, that just proves my point: these traditions create a perspective for reading the text, which leads to them extracting verses, sometimes out of context, and the verses they pick are selected to prove their point. That sounds like hiding a bias behind a claim of authority."

"Well then how would you approach scripture Eve? If we were to just throw out core doctrines then we leave people with even less guidance for reading the word. Wouldn't that lead to more misinterpretations and harm?"

"I don't think you understand my point. My concern is not about the legitimacy of these traditional doctrines, but about their resistance to even being questioned. When something is beyond the analysis of evidence, it keep people from making waves, but that still water can become intellectually stagnant."[36]

"No Eve, you don't understand MY point. Doctrines and dogma provide reassurance, traditions, and reinforcement to the belief of individuals. These principles remind the faithful that the truth remains consistent, regardless of one's personal feelings, style, or group consensus."

"You said that 'dogma provides' several benefits. However, my concern is how all of the concerns you have named are actually deeply personal concerns. They are concerns about an individuals identity within a group which dogma can dictate with a sense of fear. Fear of not being 'true' to one's group can overpower the need to be true to oneself as well. So I worry that the appeal to dogmatic claims being true can create followers who are just trying to protect their place in the world."

"Eve, that's not fair. Dogma doesn't just protect a persons place in the world. What you are implying here is an appeal to protection, and I know where that argument leads—which is an argument that I'm concerned about too. If dogma provided protection, then that protection requires enforcement. Which leads to violence and a lack of compassion. However, you can hold onto dogma without forcing those views on others."

"Adam, we both know about the long history of violent enforcement of dogma, which I want to return to as it's still an important issue and the effects of that history affect us even today. However, enforcing dogma is not always done with violent enforcement. For example, if you offer clothing or food to those in need, can you offer those services without judgment? I feel like this is what we've been talking about so far: self-care is a right for sustaining human life and it should not depend upon having the 'right' opinions. So when you to help others, but then use that as an opportunity to push your beliefs onto another, that is not collective care. That transforms a wonderful non-profit that shares responsibility for your community into something horrible. Sharing your beliefs when someone is vulnerable can be seen as blaming the individual and undermining the potential for a supportive social network."

"Eve, you can't be serious. Are you seriously arguing helping people with holistic self-care? Why would it be a bad thing to address someone physical, emotional, and spiritual needs together? Especially for those in need! Some of these people are really suffering, Eve, and when they face uncertainty and their own mortality, look at what we provide! A sense of meaning, hope, purpose, community, resources and more! How can you be against that?!"

"I'm not against helping people with their self-care—I'm questioning the consequences of combining all these together, like an all or nothing package deal. When you frame care initiatives like that you may be providing numerous advantages to vulnerable people. However, that security can be too easily conditional. It suggests that to be helped means you have to fully belong, to abandon the self and throw in support behind these dogma backed groups. Can you not see how those conditions can be enforcement with a smile? The offer sounds nice, but those who join may come to depend heavily on these systems, which is a great deal of control."

"Ohhh that is so rich coming from you. Eve, what you are describing can just as easily occur within justice movements. Just think about it: you are criticizing dogmatic beliefs, right? Well people can just as easily demand that people must believe in just the right human rights, to progress and pronouns in their direction. Then if you don't do it just right then you don't really belong. That sounds like dogma to me!"

"Adam, I am against dogma, no matter where it emerges. So yes, every group that relies behind a set of beliefs can become too rigid, exclusionary, or purist, especially when their ideology overtakes their responsibility for reflection. I'm not against having any particular beliefs, but I am against digging in, refusing to reflect, refusing to transform who we are or what we believe. That too can cause dogma."

"Okay, so then why would you be against a clearly articulated belief system? Especially when those belief systems are about consistent living, which is what self-care is all about, right? Routines, consistency, people grow within strict routines everyday."

"My issue is not with routines that promote growth. My problem, Adam, is when those strict routines are exclusionary. I'm concerned about a lack of mutual growth. For example, in a more dogmatic relationship when someone undergoes a more personal transformation that can be seen as a threat to the shared values of a dogmatic group. Which means that dogma puts restraints on transformation; where group members can only become or grow in one direction."

"Eve, how is that a bad thing? Society is constantly changing. Dogma keeps you grounded, where you can't be moved from your core values."[37]

"This just reminds me of my earlier argument about violence and enforcement. What can you do when your values cannot guide you through that changing society? Those values may have helped the group to unite before, but if those values become less useful then how do you keep your group members together? All too often, fear and violence have been used to force group cohesion."[38]

"We already talked about this point, but okay, sure. Violence happens, but that is not the only outcome. Plenty of people have walked away from all kinds of belief systems, many without violence too. Also, dogma is not as rigid as you've described it. For example, the Christian church has seen many councils, reformations, and reinterpretations that preserved the core of the belief."

"Adam, first what you just described is not dogma. Those are systems of belief that recognized the need for transformations when their dogma had to relent to change, which is the exact opposite of dogma. Replacing outdated beliefs with new ones highlights how loyalty to dogma prioritizes becoming over belonging. Which means that once a dogmatic viewpoint no longer serves a group or its people the choice to swap from one dogma to another is for the sake of preserving the group. It's akin to asserting that unity is more significant than anticipating the individuals we'll become as a collective. That decision can lead to the formation of groups that prioritize their shared interests over their personal integrity. Instead, they should consider the alternative: where the group can grow by accepting dissenting views and diverse perspectives."

"So then what do you suggest Eve; when we send our theological students off to study should they not lean upon their faith systems? Their beliefs provide a sense of belonging and self understanding. Are you suggesting that they should abandon these beliefs, and if so, what would you offer as a better replacement?"

"Let me be quite clear: no. Of course these students can lean on their faith, but my concern is about the assumption that their base of faith can be relied upon. After all, faith is not a certainty, it is a belief about what seems to be true which is an adequate cornerstone. However, every house needs maintenance, every foundation needs to be protected, but if all they have is dogma then their ability to recover from a catastrophe is compromised. I am simply saying that every students needs to prepare. Every student needs a variety of skills. Whether that be skills to maintain their values, to undergo major renovations, to rebuild when the foundation cracks, or to move when necessary."

"I agree up to a point Eve. Every individual benefits from critical thinking skills, but without continuity, without a house becoming a home, where is the motivation? What would be worth preserving, and why, and for whom?"

"Adam, I believe the question is not what to persevere, but who. We need to care more about each individual, and that starts with every individual caring for themselves. That starts with knowing who you are as an individual. When we are too quick to preserve, protect, and push a value system onto individuals we pressure conformity above individuality. Which can make the people weaker, more dependent, which means less independent, less free to know who they are and how they are valued apart from those values and roles we assign to them."

*****

Are you beginning to see how the arguments within the S.T.R.A.W.S. process can help you discern between your differences and decide on a better way through these conversations?[39] I have found that my process also provides a some comfort and growth in addition to some powerful responses to dogmatic rhetoric. Also, note how all the arguments within are interconnected to address the broader objective of every S.T.R.A.W.S. conversation: to acknowledge that dogmatic beliefs can remain based in the Bible while simultaneously emphasizing that no single individual can be the sole authority on biblical interpretation. Self-care and transformation can help us fulfill the innate desire of dogma: to better control and understand our experiences. As individuals, we are responsible for and aware of how our lives unfold.

So, before you jump the fence to mediate a dog fight with treats and training techniques, please take a moment to stretch out as we consider the start of the S.T.R.A.W.S process: self-care.[40] Self care is where you can meet that desire to insist in your own way, to care for you in the way you choose, and to think about our worldview before we face the world. In self-care, we can take care of ourselves by reconsidering our own views and approaches before our conversations turn into conflicts. This way, we can avoid getting into arguments about *why* things are the way they are. Instead, we can try to push back by digging in our heels and confronting the dogmatic standing before us.[41] However, this approach might backfire, as we could be criticized for our unwavering determination to hold onto our views.

At times, we feel like we've emerged victorious, having defeated a formidable opponent through reasoning. What we actually accomplished in moments like these was merely a series of arguments directed at a straw man that we managed to dismantle.[42] Worse still, we may have been dogmatic in the process. This implies that what seemed like a victory over dogma was merely a replacement. In these moments, discourse devolved into debate because, somewhere along the way, we inadvertently adopted the tools of dogma. How can we resist this temptation? How can we avoid being so dogmatic against dogma, which can appear condescending, driven by a desire for vengeance, appealing to fundamentalism, promoting exclusionary behavior, fueled by a fear of being wrong, or even lacking empathy?[43] The factors that drive us to employ these tactics can be attributed to various reasons. One of the major reasons is also one of the most preventable factors: a lack of self-care.

Chapter 2

How Self-Care Helps Us Look Forward

We should start preparing ourselves with self-care well in advance of such conversations. Otherwise, you might feel unprepared and emotionally exposed, which is not ideal in this situation. I should also mention that I won't be telling you how to do self-care because that's a subject thoroughly covered by many pre-existing books. I assume you already have a self-care routine. Instead, we begin with self-care to help us understand how we're both preparing ourselves for the conversations to come and forming our arguments. Self-care helps us better understand our values, which can make it easier to stick to those values during conversations. For instance, self-care can help you with:

- Form meaningful relationships and connect ideas.
- Self aware, which reminds you of your worth.
- Emotional regulation, which helps you avoid escalation and to keep you separated from the ideas you consider in a conversation.

- Staying healthy which gives you stamina and reminds you of what it takes to care for yourself. You won't as quickly betray these standards if you know how much effort you have put into caring for yourself.
- Setting boundaries which helps you keep these conversations respectful, protecting your physical and mental well being.

Can you see how conversations with the dogmatic depend upon many of the same skills that we improve with self-care? This is why self-care is our first priority. Self-care at its best is a routine of rest and recovery even while we converse with ourselves.[1] For example, have you ever had random thoughts while showering or trying to fall asleep?[2] These moments of thoughtfulness indicate how our self-care allows us to converse with ourselves. You've likely experienced this already when showering, driving to work, or any other activity in which you allow the mind to reflect. Creative writers know this phenomenon quite well. Julia Cameron has for decades taught her creative writing students the value of "morning pages", which is a routine practice of relaxing into reflection, allowing the mind to wander, and then writing down their thoughts as they emerge.[3] Anne Lamott speaks to a similar phenomenon within the writing process, where a writers best thoughts and drafts emerge after they let themselves write a shitty first draft.[4]

When we do practice self-care we are making space in which to rest, receive, and revise toward better thoughts. We want those better thoughts, both for ourselves, and for our conversation partners. You can note these better thoughts in our W.A.G. tool. Do this as youn read. Do this when you care. These routines are not just necessary to our thoughts. These routines practice a balance between listening and questioning, which will serve you well long term. We can also work through difficult thoughts by inviting conversations with friends or therapists. Do you see how these routines combine rest, develop our thoughts, and build our conversational skills? You may not see this right away. That is okay, the routine teaches the lesson over time.[5]

That lesson comes when these self-care routines help you develop one more important skill: the ability to recognize the need for self-care in others. Attentive parents learn to do this for their children. Most readers have likely developed this skill on some level already. When we recognize that someone needs self-care we notice that something is "off" with them.[6] They seem not fully present, emotionally volatile, their pace may be too fast or too slow. If you recognize these issues with a potential conversation partner then you may wonder: could I postpone a conversation or maybe point out these deficits?

These are good questions. You will recognize the answers in book three and four. For now though let's not move too quickly to the external benefits. Many of us do this in self-care, where we return to a former state of well-being and identity, which means we may miss an opportunity to grow through trans-formation. This comes up in the next book as the other side of self-care. Getting there though means we need to see how self-care connects to transformation with self confrontation. What is self confrontation? Dr. Hubert Hermans is the psychol-ogist renowned for his development of the self-confrontation method. Therapists use this method to help clients remem-ber important life events, reflect about how they feel about these events, which identify their values, and then the client re-flects upon how much they have been able to live out their val-ues. [7] As Dr. Hermans continued his research he would make an observation similar to Lamott and Cameron. Specifically, he observed how creative individuals can experience mystical ex-periences similar to spiritual individuals when they are in a receptive state, noting that "the mind [often] needs the relaxation of inner controls for new ideas to emerge".[8]

Do you see the disconnect? We often see self-care as something we do, but good self-care makes you receptive, releasing some control. Which means we stop overthinking recreative ideas and stop self-censoring so that our creative ideas can arise. Otherwise we are still clinging to our own dogged perspective, which reduces our self-care to just a routine practice where we only recognize and meet our needs. When our self care is only concerned about our needs we are ignoring the thoughts and ideas that we are reinforced with our routines. They become like ticks in the fur. To get rid of them means both a routine comb through the hair, and to be so disgusted at the thought that we could be harboring our own dogmatic views. Routine practices like these, being receptive to help, even professional help, these acts can help us recognize how we may have neglected, abandoned, or refused to love ourselves. Granted, I can see why some of us may tend to avoid self-care.

For some we fear judgment when we prioritize caring for our own needs. That is dogma against self-care. It can sound like a complaint against coddling or special treatment. For example, you may have heard this kind of pushback with phrases like "well back in my day…" or "I don't get that special treatment so why should you?"[9] Renowned sociologist Dr. Sally Haslanger is quite familiar with the meaning behind these and similar sayings. She points out how sayings like these, where one appeals to "the way things are" can just be a way of avoiding changes or criticisms.[10] So before you look for similar sayings out there, you should check for similar sentiments within. These sentiments are like a puddle that fills a pot hole: it is a gap in our thinking that may not be obvious until it causes harm. Yet with good self-care routines you can better know yourself, care for yourself, developing both resilience and enough receptivity to change your mind as needed. The prolific Audre Lorde celebrated such self-care practices as self-preservation, where we free our thinking so we can reconnect ourselves to our experiences and strengths.[11]

Scripture points to a similar experience one can have in self-care when one goes beyond the superficial reflection in the mirror to help you address how you see yourself. For example Paul wrote to the church of Corinth to encourage them to revise their thinking and consider whether they could actually see themselves clearly (1 Corinthians 13:12). Jesus did something similar within his sermon on the mount in which he spoke about how anyone can be hypocritical in judging others if they have not judged themselves first (Matthew 7:1-2)? Thus, good self-care practices will interrogate our own convictions, which is especially important if we want to point out when something is "off" with one another. Otherwise, we risk useless or harmful debates that widen the gap that separates all those who could have walked through life together (Romans 14:1; James 1:19; Proverbs 15:1, 29:22; Titus 3:9; Philippians 2:14-16).[12] We will discuss this process of reconciliation in more depth in book three. For now though, it is enough to know that the practice of self-care is strengthening and preparing us toward the possibility of reconciling conversations.

Otherwise we are inviting confrontations about our lack of accountability when we don't connect our self-care to our self confrontation. For example, Dr. Arlie Hochschild is a renowned sociologist who interviewed the ways in which numerous personal assistants felt pushed into confrontations that were not their responsibility. One assistant recounted a story saying "My employer has me buy his condoms from the drugstore and the next morning I find them used on top of his bedside wastebasket. In his mind, I don't have eyes."[13] Do you see the disconnect? The client here was using condoms, which granted is a form of self-care, but his thoughtless actions forced his assistant to have to confront a problem that the employer neglected to see. Negligence like this is just one example of the occasional need for conversations around accountability. We will look at the various tools you can use to address issues with accountability in book four. For now though it is enough to remember that intentional attention toward our self-care practices can help us in future conversations.

Good self-care then will inform how your self-worth connects you with your community. Otherwise self-care can become an assertion of our worth while giving far less consideration to the worth of others. Worse still, deficits like these set us up for failure, where we engage in conversations without appreciating the full worth of every individual. Those who know the full worth of every individual will find a balance between loving and being loved. of every individual are those who are both lovingly cared for and who love to care for others. Christians will likely recognize this language as an answer Jesus gave when he was questioned mid conversation about what is most important. So what was his answer? His answer included all of these issues and connected them to love. He asserted the need to love with your whole being, to love your neighbor *just as much* as you love yourself, because if you can't love with all your worth then you have limited how much you can extend love to others (Leviticus 19:18; Mark 12:31; Romans 13:8-10; 1 John 4:16; 1 Corinthians 13:1-13).

Worst still, if you try to push yourself, to love and give beyond how much you value yourself then you have abandoned yourself. People who do this are often known as a people pleaser, or a person with a savior complex.[14] Not to say that caring for others is bad, but when we get it out of order then we are soon to be out of order.[15] For example, have you ever conversed with someone while hungry and angry? Did you ever have to place an intricate coffee order before you've had your first sip of coffee?[16] Do you think these unmet needs could influence or even change the direction of a conversation? Yes, exactly. Unmet needs make us tired, irritable, combative, and unfocused.

These unmet needs tend to multiply outward too. Having the courage to care for yourself however means that you know your worth, that you know your rights, and that all of us must refuse to scrounge for scraps of recognition (Matthew 15:21-28; Mark 7:24-30). This reverses the situation by holding those responsible for the situation accountable. Which means that those who would damage your sense of self-worth, who would expect you to pay the price for their devaluation of you must stop monetizing your journey toward wholeness (Matthew 21:12-13; Mark 11:15-18; Isaiah 56:1-12; Jeremiah 7:4-11). For example, have you ever tried to place an intricate coffee order before having your first sip of caffeine? Perhaps you grumbled at the barista, and they may have thought about giving you decaf. Then we are tempted to misplace our frustration, pointing it towards each other. We sometimes do this to each other when we feel forced to fit into a role, a social norm, a hierarchy, or power dynamic where we devalue one another.

Can you see how your care for your mind, body, sexuality, and experiences are interconnected with your broader community (Mark 12:30-31; Romans 12:4, 13:10; 1 Corinthians 12:12-31)? You can further explore how your self-care is related to the wider community by thinking through questions like: who is meant to benefit from my conversations with the dogmatic? What typically motivates me: money, energy, time, relationships? Can I see evidence of self-care and affirmations of worth in my free time? Have I cared enough, affirming my worth by scrubbing my grumpy butt and affirming the worth of others by not bringing the wrong shit to the conversation? After all, knowing your worth is what allows you to get an advantage in upcoming conversations when you can affirm that everybody deserves the time, respect, and attention required to be cared for as an individual.

Chapter 3

Boundaries for Being

However, I uplift this right now for an important reason: if you are part of the LGBTQIA+ community then your safety and comfort need to be a priority before you have these conversations. Many LGBTQIA+ people are already familiar with how these arguments often devolve into personal attacks when we are both *the subject* of these conversations, and *subjected to* these conversations. LGBTQIA+ people don't just have a dog in this fight.[1] Like many of my peers I have too often found myself in a similar situation. I was outed, presumed a captured stray dog who is now expected to speak after I was already collared with a jingling name tag. When we dehumanize the other we create excuses for inhumane treatment. I am not some other being: I am a human being. Can we at least agree on that?

One of the ways that I show you my humanity and personal boundary is with my clothing. After all, what other creature wears clothing?[2] So when you think about my private parts, or God forbid approach me to ask me about my private parts, that is dehumanizing: you are literally ignoring my whole humanity to focus on a part of me. Also, gentlemen, especially married men, as a former man now woman with my own home grown tits, I need you to know that you're not slick.[3] I see you staring at me. My cis sisters see it too. Now I know this sounds like an unreal experience, and trust me, it feels unreal to me every time it happens. So why do people have the audacity to do something so horrible?

Well I'm not gonna go into a full lesson about the birds and the bees, except to say that we need to save the bees.[4] Both the bees and B. Judy is threatened for the same reasons: those who have too much power and ignorance assume that we are dangerous pests. So please indulge me for a moment while I appease the petulant populus about my penis: I've been distressed about my stinger too. I know how you feel. I know you don't want it in women's spaces, and believe me, this author didn't want it in her private space either.[5] Like the humble bee, I would tolerate a great deal of distress, harassment, and fear before I would finally relent, choosing to remove my stinger as a last resort. Now when a bee stings it rips their bottom off and dies, a martyr for their community.

However, when I went under the knife nobody else was hurt, the excruciating pain was mine alone to deal with, and I didn't die either. In fact, for the first time in my life I felt a depth of joy that I had never experienced before. Granted, I knew I was depressed before my surgery, but I had no idea that most people are born with this much joy! I realized this one week after my surgery, when I was healed enough to finally take a shower. As I rinsed away some blood I began to feel a sense of joy rising. I began to cry; I was overwhelmed with joy. I felt reborn, like it was the first day of my life. Like my life had now finally, fully started, after a third of my life was gone. I had no idea how much joy was never available to me, never realized the joy that cis gendered people could have from birth. For years prior I thought I knew joy. I found quite some happiness as a former husband, church pastor, and educator. people would pay me to speak. Now though, now people talk about me without knowing me.

I know why they do it though. Power and ignorance: I've been there.

Up until a couple years ago I didn't even know what a trans person was, so I couldn't even see that in myself, even when I could bear to look at myself in the mirror for more than a few moments. Now though, well now I was here. I had finally arrived, I could recognize myself in the mirror, that was me, and I was finally here. Then it hit me all at once as I stared at myself in the mirror. I was once a man. I knew about the locker room talk: I was forced to change in those locker rooms. I was sexually assaulted in the men's locker room. I would hide in the stalls, but I would still overhear these men: their locker room talk was all about sexual exploits. I suddenly felt quite vulnerable. I'm not just a woman: I'm a trans woman in these United States of America. I'm not free, I'm a target.

In that moment I stood in a gender neutral bathroom. No I don't mean a niche bathroom like those you can find in some trendy cafe or liberal college campus. No, I mean those gender neutral bathrooms that you find in every private home in America. I therefore find that most people who are against gender neutral bathrooms to be hypocritical. However, I know what they actually want, and I think what they want is valid. They want what I want, what we all want, and what we all deserve: boundaries. If you are not familiar with boundaries then I strongly recommend Dr. Tawwab's book *Set Boundaries Find Peace* who defines boundaries as those "expectations and needs that help you feel safe and comfortable in your relationships."[6] When you don't know you boundaries, you can't fully know and care for yourself.

Do you see what we have in common? Everyone deserves to be safe, to be comfortable. When you use a public restroom, do you feel comfortable? Do you feel safe? Do you like those big gaps in the door? What about the open air echo chamber that amplifies every little grunt, sniffle, or conversation? Do you get that sinking feeling when you're using a public restroom and then hear a group of people come in?[7] Me too. I don't feel all that comfortable in public in general. I'm either woman enough to get the male gaze, which is not welcome, or I feel even more unsafe when anyone wants to debate my right to be me without being harassed again.[8] So when you say you don't want men in the women's restroom, me too. I am also concerned about what men do to women behind closed doors. As a new woman I have had to learn how to protect myself from predatory men who saw my naive newness as a woman as their advantage. These same vulnerabilities are precisely why we don't want adults to date children: there is an enormous difference in power, and children can't give informed consent.

I was just three months into my new life, into my new joyful me, when I was in the shower rinsing away my own blood after I had been raped for the second time in my life. I wish I had been more suspicious of those who seemed to care about me. In hindsight their intentions were revealed. They had infantilized me. To them I was not a full person: more like a thing to chase for sport. They thought of me as a forbidden fantasy, as something shameful to want, and they acted like I should be grateful that anyone could like someone like me. I was courted, pursued, cornered like I was a presumed stray, then raped. She wasn't like my first rapist. He was assertive, violent, overpowering. Yet she was opportunistic: she waited until I she had the opportunity to ignore my every no. She, like he, ensured that no evidence would remain. So as I showered, she watched. I had been pursued for the sport, for the sexual exploit. So when I am in a state where I can legally use the women's restroom, it is only to find safety away from men, and a locking door to separate me from the smiling faces. When I dress up it is not just cute, it is both an expression of me, a part of me, and thus a boundary.

So dear reader, before you face the world, how do you prepare and take care? Do you take a moment to look at yourself in the mirror and ask yourself a few questions like: what are your boundaries? How can I ask for boundaries in a conversation? Do my boundaries define me as a whole person, and can anyone else rightfully judge those boundaries? Of course, the moment you start setting boundaries, especially if you are a marginalized person, people will start clutching their pearls because you no longer approach conversations for their judgment (Matthew 7:1-6).[9] Your boundaries, your voice, those aren't forms of rebellion. Your boundaries define you and defend your integrity. Honor them , listen to, clothe it with compassion, respect your body, that is your temple no matter what others may imagine or do to you (1 Corinthians 6:19–20). Your body is an incredible gift: please don't take it for granted. I know some people take their born with bodies for granted, I use to envy you, but now I can finally love me too. The outfit you choose is a direct representation, a literal embodiment of your boundaries and an affirmation of your sacred worth.

Over the years I've heard the dogmatic say I'm too prideful, too selfish, too revealing with my body. When I hear that I tend to go feral.[10] I think you can imagine why. So how do I respond? Well, I begin to interrogate them to the point of them becoming quite uncomfortable. What I say, all in one breath, until they insist on interrupting me, is usually something like: "okay, fair point. Clearly I don't know how to take care of myself. So what would you do with my body? I won't say no, in fact, I won't say anything! You're in control now. I'll do whatever you say—so please, go ahead, you can do whatever you want!" Most of the time I am interrupted before I even get that far. Soon they are making my arguments for me: suddenly, I'm responsible for my body? Wow! What I do with my body is up to me? What a thought! Oh, *now* you see me as a responsible adult? Do you think you've been a responsible adult champ?

I could go on but I think you see my point: their push back isn't proof that you've done anything wrong—but it could be evidence of you showing up, fully present, unapologetically caring for yourself, which offends some people who don't care for you. If we don't know someone as an individual, then we will struggle to see them as a full person. For example, trans people are less than 1% of the population, so many people may not have the opportunity to personally know a trans person. It is quite easy to generalize when you don't have access to information, and then when you see me you want access.[11] I know the feeling; it's not a good feeling. For most of my life I didn't know I was trans; I didn't know any trans people and I never thought to seek out information. That is by design though:

- The United States has a long history of attempts to erase transgender history.[12]
- The history of trans children that has been systematically erased for over a century.[13]
- There is an even longer history of erasure globally.[14]

Chapter 4

I am Loved, I am Known

So to all my LGBTQIA+ peers: can you see why our conversations and confrontations with dogma can get quite personal? Preparing for these conversations means good self-care practices that comfort, support, and realize our full authentic selves *before* it has any chance to be debated in front of us. With great self-care comes the confidence to lean in, to fully show up as a unique individual, even if the dogmatic become uncomfortable with the specifics. Ideally we would want our conversations to lead to better connections, and when we are the subject, then our authority can be our authenticity.[1] However, we need to learn how to read a situation to know whether we can safely and fully show up to these conversations. This is why the W.A.G. tool starts with safety.

After all, a conversation that leads to more connection and understanding would be easier with more equity. Yet to gradually work to achieve greater equity through conversations requires a process with more accommodations in mind. The accommodations we can accomplish with self-care, before a conversation, do more than meet our needs: they highlight the remaining needs that can be met within a supportive conversing community.[2] Dr. Brene Brown observed something similar.

Brown found that those individuals with a "sense of true belonging" are those who "commit to assessing their lives and forming their opinions of people based on their actual, in-person experiences."[3] Brown's observation here is important, but it is too easily overemphasized within self-care practices. Can we have conversations during our self-care routines that meet our social needs and should we? Yes, of course. Conversations like these though cannot fully prepare you for a conversation with the dogmatic. After all, you've probably had an incalculable number of great conversations in self-care where you built up connections with others, and then you later realized how those social skills were not sufficient for facing down a conversation with dogma. You have probably already noticed that some conversations may have supported your self-care, while other conversations, like those with the dogmatic, were emotionally and physically draining. So why are they different?

One of the main differences between these two conversations is the underlying goal behind the practice: are we reinforcing our social bonds over what we have in common, are we available for challenging perspectives, and can we balance both? When we are building community we are focusing on what we have in common, which builds the groundwork for reconciling conversations. However, when we overemphasize reconciling conversations we risk creating overly similar spaces. Spaces like these prioritize agreement, so the call for accountability and justice are seen as antisocial disruptions.[4] Accountability conversations though ask us to take social risk risks and endure discomfort as we confront sources of harm. However, when we overemphasize accountability conversations we may disillusion individuals from the community, where their individualization leads to a feeling of isolation, resentment and loneliness.

We will discuss how and when to lean into a reconciling or accountability conversations in later chapters. For now though we need to get grounded in self-care routines that help us practice a balance between the two. To practice finding this balance you need to both bond over community building, and practice showing up within these spaces with radical authenticity. I can't tell you exactly how to practice radical authenticity, but I can tell you where to find your authenticity in our next section about perspectives. Before you can go there though, I need to address what you will probably be feeling along the way toward your radical authenticity. You probably know this feeling. Have you ever felt some kind of way when two of your social groups collide? That is the feeling you need to process and deposes. Try to ease your grip on your desire to control your social environment and embrace your authentic cringe worthy selves.

Now before you get upset at me for calling you cringe worthy, allow me to position myself among you, not to appease you, but to honor the truth: we are all cringe worthy because we are all unique. I know that probably makes you uncomfortable, but sit in that headspace for a bit. What I am asking you to do is to practice embracing authenticity. Try letting go of that feeling of cringe, as that is you trying to do some impression management. No, I don't mean imitating others as a form of comedy, even though I have seen some decent imitations before. Rather when I say impression management I mean when others have an impression of you where they "think that something is true, especially when it is not...[where] something seems, looks, or feels to a particular person."[5] Remember, dogma is defined as an over allegiance to what *seems to be* true. Do you see the connection?

Authenticity opposes dogma. Which means that you will begin to fight back against numerous forms of dogma like racism, sexism, bigotry, bias, and ignorance when you can get over what others think of you, giving yourself permission to be more authentic, to be more you! Thus, self-care means caring for yourself so much that you learn to love yourself, supporting that wonderful and authentic self. When you care about you, the real you, then you will be embracing a lifelong process of transformation, where you practice being receptive to you, and to what others think of the real you, rather than trying to control their impressions of you.

*****

Working toward authenticity is a lifelong ongoing process that we will explore in greater depth in the next chapter. For now though it is enough to remember that one of goals before engaging with a conversation with the dogmatic is to embrace your authenticity, which means you "being real or true" to you.[6] When we care enough to get to know our true selves we are better equipped to reject generalizations from the dogmatic. That feeling is you talking with authority as the author of your authenticity. Which means you get to meet your needs and yourself when practicing self-care. Your self knowledge is you, the one holding individual experiences of joy and love. Which means that your conversations with the dogmatic are not limited to you playing the role of an ambassador for the whole LGBTQIA+ community. Rather, you get to name your authority, your experience, heartaches, funny stories, food preferences, and whatever else you choose to characterize yourself as a unique individual.

Which means that you got to know yourself in self-care, and embody your argument, which is helpful in several key ways! First, you are exercising your right to define yourself. Second, you get to casually highlight your right to care for your needs and wants. Finally, you are providing the kind of information people tend to bond over. This kind of information can help you move back to reconciling, toward allyship by giving your conversation partner access to a deeper sense of empathy reserved for those they know well (Matthew 25:35-40). Granted, there is no guarantee of success, but acts like these can improve your chances. Furthermore, you are giving yourself one of the greatest of gifts: greater self awareness, which is the result of exploring all the things we can learn to love about ourselves.

We of course still need to balance our desire for authenticity with the inflation of our own ego. Granted, I don't want your egos to go too far either. So how do we monitor our ego? Some will overemphasize the input of others, their criticisms, cringe, and call for compliance to be their primary guide. Others reject all forms of social inputs. We will go in depth to discuss how to balance between these tensions in the next chapter on transformations. Generally speaking though, what we want is an ego that grows to the point where we have the audacity to be authentic, to hold one another accountable, yet also humble enough to bond over our present being. Jesus exemplified this balance quite well when he was confronted by some of the egotistical dogmatists of his time. They asked Jesus to summarize the point of the biblical law. So Jesus responded by turning this question into an invitation for growth, where each of us learns what it means to love oneself, and how this self love should increase your capacity for loving others (Mark 12:29-31; Leviticus 19:17-18). Such a view means loving yourself is a prerequisite for finding a balance between loving oneself and loving others.

Now I know that is a big claim that connects the New Testament claims of Jesus with the Old Testament passages that harbor some of the most notorious of Bible bashing verses.[7] So we will spend the rest idiom of this chapter constructing a supporting argument with many other biblical passages, whose real meaning was appropriated and buried behind a dug in dogmatic.[8] To accomplish this task we will address three primary goals for the rest of the chapter. First, we will see how removing the personal attachment to a perspective can help you remove the dogma from the dogmatic. Second, how knowing oneself makes you ready with self knowledge that does not stand in the the way of justice for others. Then we will finally see how self-care mobilizes both individuals toward one another, and the community toward diasporic individuals.

Chapter 5

Considering Perspectives

One of the most common forms of resistance to self-care that I have seen is a Resist the temptation to skip or skim over self-care, as if it were a lesser priority. I have encountered numerous excuses for this temptation. For some, self-care is dismissed as selfish or boring maintenance. Others tend to tie their worth and identity to their accomplishments, so self-care is at times undervalued. If you think self-care is lazy, trivial, selfish, boring, or a waste of time then you have judged an outfit on the rack.[1] Remember what I said about clothing, how what you wear is a manifestation of your boundaries and an affirmation of knowing yourself? So I don't deny the validity of these arguments, but they must be applied to the appropriate context. In other words, self-care helps with discernment when you are considering whether you should preserve and protect your perspective. Think of it as picking the right outfit for the occasion.

For example, perhaps you can recall a time when you felt good about an outfit that now no longer looks quite as good on you. That distress is you responding to an observation. Perhaps you observed how you have transformed over time. Perhaps what you observed was an outfit made of inferior materials and is now showing signs of wear (Leviticus 19:19; Deuteronomy

22:11; Matthew 9:16).[2] Part of the frustration though is rooted in seeing oneself in a different context, like when you like an outfit at the store looks "off" once you try it on at home. Again, remember that seeing something or someone as "off" could be you sensing a need for self-care. Perhaps the outfit (boundary) is good but it's not in the right context. That observation is you noticing the same content but within a different context. Perhaps that suit is suitable when maintaining the same person. However, when your previous self-care practices no longer fit you, that is either an indication *of* change, or an invitation *to* change.

Whether it is a change in clothing, a change in perspective, or whether these changes may incidentally benefit others, please remember that these changes are for you first. The same is true when we want our dogmatic conversation partner to change their perspective. The change must be specific, contextually appropriate, and grounded as an authentic expression of their being, not just a performance where they meet a demand to say the right thing. However, the closer you get to that change the closer you will get to a volatile conversation. What we are approaching, what we are ultimately seeking to modify, is not something for us to modify, but rather it is something that each of us must accept accountability over: self awareness of our own identity.

Now I don't just mean a shallow identity, what I am referring to is what sociologists like Dr. Jonathan Turner refers to as a "core" identity.[3] One helpful way to think about this is to think of your identity, your being, as layered, like the layers of clothing, where each underlying layer is more important than the next. For example, let's undress a hypothetical doctor, a Jane Doe if you will. Jane's outer white coat indicates one of her many roles as a Cardiothoracic surgeon. Underneath that are her scrubs indicating that she is part of a group of medical professionals. Underneath that is her underwear layer, which is her social identity: here she keeps her personal beliefs about gender, ethnicity, social norms and more. Underneath all of these layers is her core identity: this is Jane. No, I don't mean her body as an object, I mean Jane as the subject. Yes, Jane has a body, but Jane is not defined by her body. Neither are you. Underneath everything is you the subject, you who are most vulnerable, you who wants to clothe yourself with dignity by seeking out "others [who] verify and confirm those identities" at the core of your being.[4]

This is why deeply personal questions from those who lack self awareness are self serving, invasive, and violating. So to my LGBTQI+ peers please remember: before you get in the middle of S.T.R.A.W.S. conversation decide who, if anyone, is allowed to undress your sexuality.[5] How you respond, if you respond, is up to you. One strategy that I have used with great success is rooted in my background as a creative writer. What I do is create a character, another Jane Doe, except I rename her and assign her a sexuality. I also assign a brief back story, age, gender, and whatever else I like. This Jane Doe is a genderless crash test dummy.

Then, I ask my conversation partner to not generalize. Instead, I ask that they talk about a lesbian I know, who is very real, her name is Jenny, and she likes fast cars. Now I know this sounds strange, dehumanizing even. However, the alternative is to be personally attacked, to have other people you know attacked, or to have the broader community be attacked. So rather than waiting for them to get personal, take action early: ask them to speak specifically about these individuals who are fine with being talked about despite not being present. In other words, they have given you prior consent to discuss them. This strategy holds numerous benefits. For example:

- I can stay more present in the conversation, even when my dogmatic conversation partner trys to push past Jennys boundaries.
- My conversation partner now has more accountability because their comments must be being personally directed toward a "friend" of mine.
- This strategy also shifts the power dynamics a bit: your "friend" is now part of the conversation.
- You can also write a cast of different dummies on your W.A.G. tool to help you remember each one. Then your "community" is visible to the dogmatic, easier to remember, and your actual community is safe as they are not part of the conversation.
- Your conversational dummies can take on whatever identity they need. This keeps your conversation flexible, yet accountable. After all, you don't have to personally know us dolls, nor our names, to defend us.
- I once used this to crowd test a couple names before my name change.
- Your resilience can increase if this are a source of amusement for you. For example, some of my crash dummies were named after politician's, and another was the dead name of a friend of mine who volunteered their dead name.
- This also gets ahead of the tired "gay friend" defense, which is often just a way for the dogmatic to avoid accountability or criticisms.

Now they could refuse the request. If they do, then perhaps they would agree to keeping our conversation topics less personal, where personal statements are only "I" statements about oneself and not about anyone else. So feel free to start your statements with "I feel" as that is a good tool. After all, we are the authoritative source of how we feel, especially when we are mid conversation. However, appealing to outside sources to support other "I" statements tend to reveal a different problem. They may sound like accountability over ones dug in beliefs, but such statements tend to distance the speaker from their various social groups who support their dug in position. When we don't callout these "I" statements they solidify into perspectives they may seek out quotes from the Biblical canon or citing outside research to support their bias.

All of us are susceptible to these tendencies. These tendencies are not new as researchers have been studying this phenomenon for decades. Dr. Henri Tajfel noted how even "the mere awareness of the presence of an out-group is sufficient to provoke intergroup [competition] or discriminatory responses on the part of the in-group."[6] This is why our conversational crash dummies are helpful: they can stand in for those "I believe _____" statements that move too fast toward an group allegiance, which can leave too much space for harmful discriminatory responses. These issues are further compounded when the Bible is appropriated outside of it's context, especially when our conversation partner may not appreciate, have access to, understand, nor care what another person's holy book may say.

I expect by now you may have thought I've been hypocritical. Are you wondering why I have downplayed the dogmatics appeal to protect their community while uplifting a tool in which you do the same thing to protect the LGBTQIA+ community? My answer is quite simple: comparing these two communities is a false equivalency. For example, think about the Black Lives Matter movement, which was a community response to the erasure of black lives. Then the dogmatic disciples of superiority would both deny the inequity to support their in group, yet use their inequitable power to appropriate the cry for black lives.

Worse still the majority in group would erase the term "Black" from a slogan they criticized, only to appropriate that slogan to support the same unreformed system that had erased black lives and caused the original outcry. Which brings me back to my main point: self-care can preserve your personhood and protect your own perspective. However a change in perspective does not mean that you lack protection, preservation, or care for oneself, no matter how it may seem. If anything you should strive to preserve and protect the perspective of the people within the Bible. Otherwise we misappropriate, generalize, and assume to understand the lived experiences of those who can no longer speak. So when I make up people for a conversation I do it to protect those vulnerable peers who are still with us.

Chapter 6

Integrity, Intent, and Impact

Yet when the dogmatic say "I believe _____", I begin to wonder: have they erased any part of that biblical characters identity for their own purposes? What I mean is: what are their intentions, are they speaking with integrity, and how will their words be impactful? I know this raises the importance and emotional intensity of a conversation. Also, yes, we can have another conversation to ask questions, to clarify what we mean, to heal from harm, and to have one last conversation to say goodbye. Each of these conversations have intentions that seek to balance our integrity with the impact of our words. Which means that every conversation is an opportunity, and ideally a mutual opportunity. So how can we ensure that our conversations provide a mutual opportunity?

We do this by honoring the intent, or purpose, of a conversation. We do this by keeping the subject in the middle of the conversation. To keep the center we must mutually surround it with two things. First, surround the conversation with your integrity, which means protecting the whole being of others and ourselves. Second, we respect the impact of words, as these hold the power to affect and evoke thoughts in others. Now imagine these three together in a conversation. Can we offer the respect, the time, and the resources needed for everyone involved? In other words, if you had the chance to speak with little chance of being interrupted, can we honor that opportunity to speak? Most people would assume they can. However, in my experience I have noticed a more nuanced answer emerge. As an example, here is a conversation space in which many of us have had the discomfort of attending: a funeral.

I have organized and presided over quite a few funerals over the years. Funerals have a way of bringing out arguments about the purpose of the service.[1] I have seen and mediated over many such arguments that should have been conversations. The arguments varied, but the core was often the same. Those with grief and grievances end up debating when they replace a common intent with an uncommon ideal of their own imagining. They focus on what they think as a perfect funeral, often to distract them from the grief of realizing that there is no such thing. So how do I move them closer to saying yes to a plan for the funeral? By telling them no. When I say no, I am saying no we will never say everything we need to, and no the circumstances will not be perfect. What I bring to the conversation is the painful reality of death, which is the ultimate no.[2]

In that moment I center the reality of death, not to give it power, but to remind us of our common purpose in the conversation. I force us to face and surround that uncomfortable subject together. You can see the shift when it happens, when we can zoom out together from the tragedy of the day and together surround grief with beautiful moments. I have witnessed the raw beauty of funerals many times. Like how we see the seasons change, when spring fades, the flowers die, but we saw the flowers bloom.[3] Yes, some flowers had a full life cycle. Others were cut in peak bloom. Some never got to bloom.

Yet when we circle around the felt loss, around that hole, we are together surrounding a gap in which life once stood. That hole, like a black hole, is both destructive when it pulls us in too close, and yet it has a powerful gravity.[4] Death attracts a gathering of raw and rare relating.[5] We bring flowers, friends, family, faith, feelings, and food to flock around a funeral. All of this is gathered, brought into a conversation space, where the topic is a matter of life and death. In that gathering we try to stay present, grounded in reality before we face the reality of a loved one being lowered into the ground.

So we gather to exchange thoughts with an agreed upon intent: to both look back for the integrity of their whole being, and to keep look forward so we can see how their life continues to impact us even today. We confront that space with some comforts, some discomforts, and conversations. In that space full family systems are on display. Then, as we gather to listen from those who would stand up before others to provide a eulogy, to make a statement about the missing life that we have gathered to grieve over together, in that setting we see the culmination, the difficulty of balancing all of the demands of that day. Those who stand to speak gather their wits, along with a collection of anecdotes, bits of wisdom, occasionally song lyrics, as they try to speak to so many gathered people spanning various cultures, and experiences. The task of the eulogy is to care for, honor, and remember a whole being; that is a large undertaking.

However, you should be somewhat familiar with these tasks because you do something quite similar in self-care. Do you see the connection? Self care is the prep work that allows you to fully attend the conversation task. For example, my beloved former church members would anticipate the self-care needs of those in grief by planning meals, stocking the church with tissues, or passing out bottles of water. These simple acts help us to find moments to slow down, to take care of yourself, and then to rejoin the moment with renewed intentions. These physical tasks are there to help ground us in reality, to keep us from jumping to conclusions or judgments.[6] Otherwise, we become like the dog guarding the door.

When the conversation task comes knocking we need to be well prepared, grounded, empathetic, knowing who we are, the boundaries we have set, and honoring the intent behind the conversation event.[7] We don't appropriate, abuse, or misrepresent anyones perspective. Rather, with permission, we seek to understand, to honor their vulnerability, to acknowledge how our loss and their absence are barriers to our understanding. We admit when we are lost, we admit our ignorance, and the messy parts. We also name our hope, the triumphs, the laughter, the memories that brought us close, that still brings us close, and we in that space we can also reflect upon what death has not taken from us.

If we are not both moving around the subject together then we risk getting dug in, where one of us is centered and we refuse to move together. Sometimes these moves are justified, which I will discuss in just a moment, but first let's talk about when these movements are more dogmatic. Here again, one of the ways to tell the difference is to ask yourself: what are the intentions of the one being centered? Do they malign the remembrance of whole lives, choosing instead to make this yet another day about them? For example, I once had to set a eulogy back on course after a friend of the deceased turned their reflections away from the intent of exchange, choosing instead to share what they knew about the deceased porn preferences. When he made that shift away from what he had originally written down he made the choice to betray our agreed upon social intentions. This is one of the reasons why I encourage you to keep a written W.A.G. statement as it makes your intentions clear, and helps you stay accountable to your own stated intentions.

Otherwise, these shifts in intentions, which are already quite subtle, can be that much harder to recognize. Now, I did not immediately jump in when he made a double entendre about how his now 'stiff' friend. However I did stand up at that point and in the next moment I was ready to interrupt him when he moved from grief to grievance. In that moment he centered himself, which means he was no longer centering a wholesome remembrance of his friend.[8] I could see how he was no longer addressing the grieving friends and family. That was the shift in intention: from caring about us to caring for just himself. In that moment I used one of my accountability tools which I first learned from my mom.

The technique is fairly straightforward: when someone is betraying the intent behind a conversation you can recognize it as a teachable moment and work back from an F grade to an A grade. I remember the technique as an acronym: F.E.D.C.B.A. which stands for Feel, Disrupt, Care, Boundary, and Ask. For example, here is how I implemented it with this rouge eulogist:

1.   Feel: I was staying in touch with the emotions I had connected to the intent and purpose of the exchanges of the day. Your first clue about the change in intentions is being able to detect when something feels 'off'.
2.   Evoke: If something feels off, then ask yourself: what words felt 'off' to me and what did they make me think about? For example, when he said 'stiff' something micro came to mind, like a tiny red flag.[9]
3.   Disrupt: Up until now I was listening with emotional availability, watching how their words impacted and evoke. Once I knew that his intentions were self centered I spoke up. So I turned on my personal mic to say "excuse me" and that was all I needed to say to disrupt his statement.

4. Care: I then immediately identified what we needed to care about by restating the intent behind the day. I reminded him that "we are here to grieve over our mutual loss" and I could tell he had already realized how he had made a mistake. However, I didn't leave him standing there unsure of how to proceed. That's a C grade effort, so I continued.

5. Boundary: I then set a boundary, even though I did not call it a boundary in that moment. I told him that we want to hear some words for comfort, and community as we remember the deceased.

6. Ask: I then give him back his turn to speak by asking him a question that met those agreed upon intentions. I had an advantage here as I saw his written eulogy before he went up front so I asked him a question about his next topic: "Could you share with us one of your earliest memories?"

With that he wiped away his tears, and with a smile he shared a story about having to share his toys with his new friend. What he was going through in that moment was familiar to me as I had seen this earlier in life. In my childhood home my mom ran a daycare center. I often had the immense privilege of watching my mom respond to a crying child, where she would redirect their energy form a center of attention to an investigation about their missing care needs. When a child cries we ask them what is wrong, we look for injuries, offer a snack, or check their diaper. However, she would only start with guessing when it was a baby crying. For the older kids, who had the ability to articulate their needs, she would lead them in a problem solving conversation. She would ask them what happened, encouraging the child to use their words and tell the story of how we got here. She had innumerable strategies like these, all while juggling various demands with love, grace, and an assertive voice.

She was my first heroine. Like a flying superhero she had her arms always outstretched for an embrace when I came home from school crying, which happened quite often. She would ask me what happened and I did my best to explain my perspective even though I didn't yet have the words to name a transgender experience. All I knew was that my masculine peers would harass me and sexually assault me for being too feminine. Meanwhile, my feminine peers were raised to be more fearful, more suspicious, so most of them could not look past my masculine exterior. Which means that many of my early childhood conversations were confrontations, like a high stakes social game. Granted, I did occasionally find the rare exceptional being to befriend. I would treasure their conversations and guard them with everything I could bring, just like mom. So I would watch my mom to figure out how her powers worked.

Many years later I would come across Dr. Daniel Siegel and Dr. Tina Pyne Bryson's book *The Whole-Brain Child*. It was there, in book two of their work that I recognized one of the many techniques that my mom had been using for decades. They refer to it as the "name it to tame it technique", which helps children name their emotions, identify the problem, come up with possible solutions, and then try different solutions.[10] So when I see an adult re-center themselves in a mutual conversation I recognize the shift: they want me to care about their request as they center themselves. Sometimes that demand is justified, like when we call for an ambulance or change the topic to discuss dinner plans. At other times though, it is a way to colonize a conversation toward a self centered exchange. You can learn to detect these shifts too.

Start by examining where you place your attention when doing your self-care routines. Then notice how your attention shifts when a conversation starts. Pay attention to these shifts as you engage in self-care practices. Over time you will learn to recognize these as shifts in intentions, shifting between others and ourselves. Granted, not all of us are comfortable with switching to and staying within a plural perspective. This is vital though to our conversations and you can improve these skills over time. After all, we need a more plural perspective in social settings like conversations and we even need this perspective when we are reading the words of another. You may have begun to do the same thing with my own words. Perhaps you want me to get to the point, which is the point where my integrity honors your attention by giving you some impact tools to use for your upcoming conversations, as that was our agreed upon mutual intentions correct? Well, have I made my point? I believe I have, but beloved please let me be blunt as I don't want you to miss a bigger point: the dogmatic do something quite similar with the Bible.

Chapter 7

Self-Care, Not Self Centered

For example, the core of the Bible features a life account of Jesus, along with quite a few more books covering the before and after. So when you enter into a conversation please pay attention to what is centered as the topic. After all, we all have our backgrounds and biases, which I will discuss in more detail in the second book of this series about transformation. For now though, I invite you to begin this work by to identifying some of the more common biases. As you work through the list, think about how the dogmatic, I the author, and even you may have been led by bias. Here are just some of the biases:

- **Present centered bias**: a bias toward our moment in time, where we project our present beliefs, values, and social norms onto the past.[1]
- **Egocentric bias**: a personal bias, where we reflect our personal needs and perspective, thus making the Bible about their specific life.[2]
- **Ethnocentrism bias**: a cultural bias, where we assume that our own culture is represented in a text that pre-dates our own.[3] For example, when we replace the Bible's collectivism with modern individualism.

- **Confirmation bias**: a bias of self protection, when we seek out evidence to support what we already believe but ignore contrary evidence.[4]
- **Cognitive ease bias**: a bias that leans away from hard work, perhaps even opting out of exegetical study, as that is easier or more comforting.[5]
- **Availability heuristic**: a popularity bias, which is when we lean upon the more popular views or common interpretations of the Bible.[6]
- **Narcissistic hermeneutic**: a combination of several of these biases, which is the tendency to see yourself as a main character within the text, thus ignoring the historical context and the original authors intentions.[7]

Do you see any familiar biases that you may have fallen into? I know I have fallen for all of these at some point in my career and I'm sure I did not catch all of these biases before passing them along. However, awareness is an important step toward fighting against our own dogma. These biases also tend to emerge when we neglect our self-care. For example, we may lean into a cognitive ease bias when we are tired. When we feel attacked in a conversation against dogma we may let our confirmation bias or ethnocentric bias to lead our defense. When we want words of encouragement for the day we may be led by a present centered bias. These tendencies are yet another reason why we start with self-care.

Otherwise we may risk misappropriating an ancient body of text, digging in to carve out our points, and to stand in a hole that we built.[8] All of us are capable of doing this very dogmatic behavior in conversations. When we do this though our conversation falls apart: the original intent, major points, and context are at best misunderstood, if not thrown away. For example, what if I told you that the Bible promises a guardian angel to you, one who will keep you from harm if you just trust God (Psalm 91:1-12)?

I could claim that you are invincible based on these verses, if that was the original intent. However, all I am actually doing is pulling verses out of context and misinterpreting them. Satan is accused of doing this outright when he misquoted the same verses in an attempt to encourage Jesus to jump off a temple roof to test whether he was in fact protected (Matthew 4:5-7). Can you see how the text can be taken out of context to support abusive behaviors? We don't want to do that. We will instead do our best to avoid jumping to similar conclusions, especially in those places where Jesus didn't jump.[9] However, it is not enough for us to avoid making the same mistakes: we must have some concern for those who could be convinced to jump in the bed with dogma without understanding the inherit risks, which is a task that Jesus would frequently take on.[10]

For example, consider the time when Jesus and his posse of apostles would pause their journey for some self-care by grabbing some whole grain snacks from a nearby field (Luke 6:1-2).[11] Note two things: first, their actions are not an act of theft nor poor planning. After all, Jesus has allegedly turned water into wine before, and he is believed to be part of the three-in-one trinity of God, a God who once provided manna in a food desert (Exodus 16:1-5; John 2:1-11). So we may be tempted to criticize Jesus here for refusing to make it rain snacks, but again, that is a misreading of the character of Jesus.[12] Here again, recall the earlier story where Satan misquotes scripture: in that same story Satan made the same argument. When Satan makes this argument Jesus offers a response rooted in his context. Jesus points out that he came here, to the desert, to fast on purpose, and to face down this devils temptations (Matthew 4:1-2). Jesus response reveals multiple points at once (Matthew 4:2-4):

- Jesus has clear intentions, he claims to be the living word, which means he will fulfill the word. For Jesus, this is a matter of integrity.
- When Satan questions Jesus divine identity, Jesus quotes a verse addressed to human men. He doesn't have to prove his humanity, his divinity, or anything else. His intent was to fulfill scripture.
- When the devil tries to gaslight him into a response, Jesus refuses. He knows that his words are impactful and not self serving.

So let's return to the whole grain story: why can the disciples just take some grain from the edge of a field that doesn't belong to them? Our confusion here could be rooted in a present centered bias. When we read it within its context we know that the one word answer is justice. The longer answer is this: when they pause to rest they have a reasonable expectation for hospitality as a traveler, because at the time that was a common law practice. Moreover, it is also a biblical law from Leviticus, yes, that Leviticus.

We will soon return to Leviticus in context to see how many more ways it advocates for self-care by connecting the community to care resources. First though, yes, in Leviticus it forbids the lords of the land from reaping everything that they sow. By law they are expected to leave some grain behind so that the poor and travelers can have something to eat (Leviticus 23:22). So when these traveling disciples stop to take some grain from the edge of the field, they are enjoying the generosity of a local farmer who follows biblical law (Deuteronomy 23:24-25; Matthew 12:1-8).

However, the dogmatic Pharisees of this story, who are supposed to know their holy texts as leaders, can't even recognize Jesus who is supposed to the living word of God who is following the biblical law (Matthew 23:29-31; John 1:1-11, 5:39-40; Acts 13:27). They are supposed to know that law, after all, the law is written within their holy book. Sadly, this makes sense: they are the dogmatic people of their day. They are abusing their power to serve themselves, by disregarding the original intent of the word, which compromises their integrity because they are abusing the power of their position to bring a harmful impact to their words. Sound familiar? These Pharisees espouse false information by misrepresenting the disciples efforts toward self-care as an act that breaks the Sabbath law, which ironically is a law about self-care (Exodus 20:8-10; Leviticus 23:3; Matthew 12:2; Hebrews 4:9)! Again, these pharisees are not actually concerned about enforcing the law, that is just their cover story. What they want to do is abuse their power, to weaponize their beliefs, to criticize others and defend themselves with the same text.

They hate how the disciples have found a loving community of care outside of their organized religion because that community is outside of their control (Matthew 27:1, 18; Mark 2:16). That threatens their power. These pharisees want to stretch their authority to cover the disciples, Jesus, and the broader community of farmers.[13] Think about this from the perspective of the pharisees: if you wanted to reclaim power over free people, what would you do? Would you be concerned about those practices that raise awareness, communal care, and the sharing of resources, which are all ways of caring for individuals?

Let's shift our focus from the Bible for a moment to think about this problem from a modern perspective. Think about an employee who submits a request for time off for self-care. Now, what is the difference between a manager who is annoyed at you, as if they only seem to tolerate your request for time off. Now compare that with the manager who knows why your requested time off is important to you, your loved ones, and your community of coworkers. What does this second manager know that the first manager does not? Perhaps they know that our days of self-care allow us to pause, to remember, to be grateful, to find community, to identify any needs yet to be met, and enjoy some festive recreation (Leviticus 23:1-44; Isaiah 58:13-14; Luke 7:31-35; John 2:1-11; Colossians 2:16-17; Nehemiah 13:15-22).

Chapter 8

Love > Bias,
Burnout, or Bigotry

W hen we prioritize self care then we have normalized taking the time to humanize ourselves by caring for our
needs. Can you imagine where we would be without being free
to meet our needs? These self care routines then are more than
thoughtful moments: they help us navigate the give and take of
challenging conversations with love.[1] After all, we have already
seen how self care can help us to reaffirm our identity, sexuality,
opinions, and favorite coffee order. We can slow down to appreciate the work and life experiences of others when we know
how to restore our endurance so that we can overcome our own
biases. For example, consider the different responses one may
have when they read an information pamphlet about HIV/AIDS.
Those with a limited understanding will respond with disgust,
stigmatizing the disease and those who are afflicted. While others receive a helpful message: negate the spread of disease by
taking care of yourself and your community before they
burnout.[2]

The book of Leviticus touches on similar themes related to
self care, so it also suffers from a similar division of reactions.
Which makes sense when you examine the events that led up
to the creation of Leviticus. Specifically Leviticus was intended

to instruct the Levitical priests on how to establish and care for a community of former slaves, who carry with them generations of trauma (Exodus 1:11; Leviticus 19:33-34, 25:38-43, 26:45). Such a lack of self care, especially with a history of atrocities committed over several generations, would compound with present day trauma.[3] Over the generations they were bought, sold, abused, forced to procreate, and to labor under the laws of their captors (Exodus 1:13-14). Now imagine what it would take to move from no control to full self determination, from being possessed as an object to having possessions as a subject.[4]

What would you do with your new found freedom when all you've known is slavery? Keep in mind, someone once owned your whole identity. Now though you can adopt, adapt, or wholly reject your former identity, so who would you be? Keep in mind, you were once forbidden from organizing into big groups, but now you can for the first time build a beloved community. If you were the leader of such a group, what would you say to the people? The book of Leviticus addresses these concerns, which are quite similar to the experiences of the formerly enslaved of the United States. For example:

- Their precarious lives are experienced and supported from moment to moment (Leviticus 19:9-10, 23:22, 25:35-37).[5]
- They had to balance between reclaiming their freedom to act in their own self interests and justice for their neighbor (Leviticus 19:15-18, 25:35-43).[6]
- They must reject the culture of the enslaver and reclaim a culture that affirms their full worth (Leviticus 18:1-5; 20:22-24).[7]
- Every leader must carefully consider their use of power (Leviticus 4:3-12).[8]

Thus, the book of Leviticus provides thoughtful instructions for Levitical priests who are facing an incredibly difficult task. One of their less obvious tasks though was to re-establish habits that affirm every individual's worth, in part by providing healthcare to the community, and awareness about various health risks to the community. These levitical priests possessed a knowledge about healthcare that they gained by observing the consequences of various actions and practices (Leviticus 18:24-25). Observations like these emerged over numerous generations, which were then shared with the community to warn them about the risks involved with certain acts of intimacy (Leviticus 18:6-17). Yet, when we read Leviticus with our various biases and ignorance unchecked we end up misunderstanding their role as stewards of the community.

So when you consider all of these factors together, like the historic context of the people, and the biases we bring, we can begin to see that Leviticus is not condemning the homosexual orientation (Leviticus 18:22). Rather, this verse is rightfully interpreted as a statement against pedophilia. We know this for a variety of reasons:

1. This verse is framed around a command: don't do what the Egyptians and Canaanites did (Leviticus 18:3, 24, 30). Which makes sense; many of the ancient Near Eastern region had a vibrant verbal tradition, which helped them to share and permeate similar laws throughout the region. These include Hittite Codes, the Code of Hammurabi, various Middle Assyrian Laws, and Ugaritic texts, which had some striking similarities.

2. The Hittite Codes is one such example, which also predates the book of Leviticus by several centuries, and it states that the concern is about men having sex with their sons. Recurring parallels like these across multiple historic

texts have prompted scholars like Dr. Susanne Scholz to call for a "fresh debate" to fight back against the tendency to lean "on the literal meaning of the Bible."[9]

1.   Now, before you object, yes this would mean a forbiddance against incest. Which yes of course incest is horrendous. However, two things: first, even before verse 22 Leviticus already forbids incestuous relations with relatives, including related sons and daughters (Leviticus 18:6-17). Second, the sexual act being described in verse 22 is forbidding a sexual act the Israelites likely witnessed in ancient Egypt, and the average age of that population was just 20.[10] Thus, these acts sexual assaults upon vulnerable males could be referring to pedophilia, incest, or rape.

2.   When verse 22 says male it is a translation of the Hebrew word zā◈ār, which just means the male gender, which includes infants[11]. Earlier in Leviticus the same word zā◈ār is used to describe a mother's newborn baby boy (Leviticus 12:2). Zā◈ār is also used later to tell the males to pay more to the temple, and those zā◈ār vary in age from vulnerable children to vulnerable adults (Leviticus 27:1-8).

3.   So why then is the Bible filled with references against homosexuality? Well, one of the reasons is discussed by researchers Kathy Baldock and Ed Oxford who were featured in *1946: The Mistranslation That Shifted Culture*, in which they investigate how a mistranslation led to the addition of the term "homosexual" into the Bible.[12]

4.   Finally, remember again that the worldview of the people of Leviticus is informed by their experiences with enslavement. evidence for the brutalization and sexual assault of enslaved children is not secluded to ancient his-

tory. The United States still needs to reconcile with their own brutal history of pedophilia of the enslaved.[13]

Our biases and worldview conversations tend to be strongly established within our own worldview. So when conversing with the dogmatic remember how the intersection of race, gender, age, sexuality, and social systems are all important lenses. Paul was a former dogmatic who would eventually recognize the diversity of experiences and worldviews among Jesus followers (Galatians 3:28). Even Jesus himself would note how our varied perspectives should inform how we speak to one another (Matthew 15:21-28; James 2:1-4). And if anyone wants to lean too heavily into the literal teachings of Paul or Jesus, then maybe remind them that such an approach leads to some rather sexist claims that continue to ignore the labor of women who helped them with self care, which were vital to their ongoing ministry efforts.

Chapter 9

The Social Impact
of Self-Care

To see how your self-care impacts the community just look at how social reform emerges after many of the miracle narratives. One such narrative recalled the social impact that followed after Jesus heals ten lepers. Note first the social standing of these leapers: they are living in a quarantined space outside of their community, where they care for themselves, provide solidarity for one another, and fulfill the law of Leviticus (Leviticus 13:9-33). Yes, *that* book of Leviticus. The very same book which so many anti-LGBTIA+ Christians love to quote is also interpreted by Jesus, except Jesus followed the law by connecting self-care and community together. When he heals the ten leapers he is fulfilling the biblical mandate by telling these lepers to return to the priests of their community, who then perform a health screening as they are welcomed back to their caring community (Leviticus 13:9-33; Deuteronomy 24:8; Luke 17:11-14).

So even Jesus understood how his position of power was defined by an interpretation of scripture that recast leaders as servants (Matthew 20:28; Mark 10:45). Like Jesus, these Levitical priests also servants of the people who screened for social contagions like hate, selfishness, and vengeance (Leviticus 19:18;

Mark 12:30-31). These community leaders understand the importance caring for every community member. To say the Levitical priests cared for the temple is to say they cared for both a place and a people (Leviticus 10:10-11, 16:16; 1 Corinthians 3:16-17). Dogmatic believers who wish to object here should remember that Christians are supposed to believe in abundant grace. Which means that those who identify as tailgaters of Jesus should not be so concerned and full of judgement as to follow you so closely.[1] They are to back off your bumper for the sake of love, and to care for every life, even those they may identify as enemies (Matthew 5:44, 1 Thessalonians 5:15, Romans 12:20).[2] Furthermore, they should remember how their own book demands for all inclusive care. Which means that self-care is just the beginning of what dogmatic believers should have been concerned about all along.

For example, Jesus would balance his public service and ministry with self-care. He would often take time away from the public, even from his disciples, to meditate in prayer (Matthew 26:36; Mark 1:35, 14:39, Luke 5:16). Now I know some may wish to push back here by pointing out that prayer is not the same as meditation. If you are one of those individuals then please consider the following: the christian God forms a trinity, correct? Which means that the Christian God is an inseparable three in one entity: Jesus is God, God is the Holy Spirit, and the Holy Spirit is Jesus, creating three in one (Genesis 1:26; Isaiah 44:6; Matthew 28:19; John 10:30, 14:9-16; 1 John 5:7-8; 1 Corinthians 12:4-6; Revelation 22:13). So when Jesus prays to God, Jesus is speaking, introspecting, and listening to themselves. Therefore, Jesus prayers are moments of self-reflection and self-care. They are making opportunities to be still, thoughtful, and focused on the connection with oneself (Psalm 23). These restorative moments were invaluable to individuals like Jesus who must anticipate what they have to sacrifice, the temptations they must refuse, even when in seclusion with nobody else watching, they continued to model justice as leaders who cared for themselves and others together (Leviticus 19:15; Matthew 4:1-11; Luke 22:39-46).

Self-care moments like these also build self knowledge and help you to become more intentional about what you experience in life. Try raising your awareness and intentionality with questions like these:

- What motives do I share with the people in my life?
- Do their contributions honor me as a unique individual?
- How well do they know me? Who knows me by my heart? My appearance? My resume?
- How much effort do people invest into knowing me before they choose to impact my life?

Questions like these can help you to see and meet your needs in self-care. Failing to address questions like these though is a bit like skipping a meal before donating blood: so wash up, eat, drink, and replenish with some quality time (Matthew 26:17-30; Mark 14:18-26; Luke 22:19-22; John 13:1-17). Consider for example how communities of faith will often bond over the sacraments of baptism and communion, which are acts of communal self-care. Yes many Christians will adhere to a schedule and set of circumstances for these acts. These acts routinize holistic care as an integral part of building community.

For example, communion should exemplify the mutual satiation of oneself and others, like the feeling you have when enjoying a community meal. Moments like these help to connect our self-care to our community. Baptism highlights similar themes: it is at least a ritual of holistic cleansing that highlights the care due to that individual, whose well being is bound within a community. These themes repeat throughout scripture by setting similar expectations that connect your self-care to the broader community (1 Corinthians 11:27-32; Acts 2:38; Matthew 6:25-27).

Thus, self-care is accomplished in various contexts, like when we are alone during extended time away from our community, or when our self-care practices require us to move between different social groups. These different contexts can help us get acquainted to differing needs, specialized care, and in some extreme instances we care is provided under quarantine where we would separate people into specialized centers or hospitals. Note how each context is conducive to a different kind of care and how the practice of moving people to different contexts for better care, with the community in mind, is not a new idea (Leviticus 13:4-5, 21, 26-27, 31, 50, 54). However, the dogmatic tend to ignore how our context of care shifts so they often miss the intent of these texts. They instead abuse the text to perpetuate their own hatred and disgust against LGBTQIA+ people.

So before we come anywhere close to a conversation with the disgusted dogmatic, please slow down, get in tune with your senses, and replenish a bit. Take some time to reflect or meditate. Try imagining your life experience as a pool of water: how would you slow the flow of life experience? How could you get that pool of water to be still so that you can better reflect and process? Set a routine for this: find a quiet and safe setting where you can explore those thoughts. For some, you may find routine therapy to be the best route here. For others they may like going to the gym, goat yoga, or longer showers with loud music. Whatever works best for you; just make sure you have a routine for reducing mental clutter and stress. That way, you will have more clarity and presence of mind when engaging with the difficult discussions to come.

Chapter 10

Return to the Heart

Now as we close our time together I want to offer you both some final words of encouragement, and a reminder that what is to come is something you can handle. Please remember that dogma cannot hold complete power over you because it cannot understand you. Dogma cannot apprehend who you are, how you love, and why you care so much, so it distorts you. It flattens your story because it cannot understand you, so it attacks your humanity. And then it demands that you defend your existence in a language designed to erase you.[1] Be the queer, trans, neurodivergent, disabled, deconstructed, othered, or allied person who leads a life so full that you cannot fit in to their narrow box called "normal."

Please also remember that the S.T.R.A.W.S. process is not a replacement box, it is just a tool. Tools hold no power unless they can serve as an extension and utility for the wielder. I will continue to hone this tool, to make it the best it can, because I know that conversation tools like these, if they are useful, are being invited into sacred spaces. I am motivated by both the privilege of equipping you with whatever I can, and further motivated by my dream to see no more dogma. I have pursued that dream long enough to see dogmatic conversation partners recognize that passion within me, and then turn on me to to seek my erasure.[2] Out of necessity I have found a way to respond, and that response begins with self-care, which is about so much more than pampering![3] It's about refusing to become the brittle, performative version of yourself that dogma demands.[4]

Self-care helps you remember your softness when the world wants you sharp, silent, or shamed.[5] It's how you stay vivid when they try to render you in grayscale.[6] It's not a retreat from justice—it's your return to wholeness.[7] Again and again. Dogma's worst trick is not cruelty—it's compression by convincing you to cut away at your whole being to meet their standards.[8] I've been there; I know the hurt that comes from conformity. When you stop laughing too loudly. When you avoid saying "I love you" to your partner in front of certain people. When you restrain your joy because someone might think it's "too much." Then slowly, you start to shrink emotionally, socially, spiritually. Not because you lost the argument, but because the atmosphere taught you that your fullness was unsafe.[9]

Self-care says fuck that, I am me, I will always be me, I will always care about me because I mean more than whatever meanness you face. So eat whatever nourishes you. Dance in your kitchen and don't explain why. Dump your messiest self into a journal where your inner critique is not invited. Text your loved ones something absurdly honest and encouraging. Do it now while you're thinking of them—and let them know! Then whatever works well for you, let it be a routine where you feel and exist without the need for protective boundaries. Get naked if you have to, just be sure it's someplace where you don't have to check who might be watching. With every experience may you find elation, joy, the sacred truth of you which deserves to be and belong. Let these experiences fill you, fuel you, and inform you of what is worth fighting for.

Remember, when you tend to yourself well, you're not avoiding the conversation—you're choosing what is worth more.

You're refusing to be turned into a lesson or a spectacle. You're claiming the quiet rebellion of being a whole person in a world that wants less, or just segments to get you bent out of shape, just to fit a false theological mold.[10] Except you alone get to mold your life and character. For you are more than the roles cast in someone else's cautionary tale: you are a full human being right now, as you are. So be soft or weird. Laugh, cry, or hold your boundaries. Bring all of you as you live out your whole story, a story that you are happy to share with those who have arms to hold all of you, or take your whole self with you if you encounter those who refuse to even respect your name.[11] Dogma wants you to perform palatability, but self-care is your time to decide who is in your audience. That's the difference.

So let yourself be complex, unedited, inconvenient, boring, brilliant, or just be fucking human. Then when the dogmatic heckle you for your silence, your tears, your proof, your patience, or your composure you get to say: "I'm not here to beg you to embrace my humanity; I've already embraced me.[12] So now I'm going to call back my security, because your insecure ass is no longer welcome." That is self-care helping you recover your voice after you've encountered your full self, after you have heard your own heartbeat and are glad that it beats for you.[13] Yes the dogmatic may refuse to change their heart. Yes the conversation may get your heart racing. When that happens, please remember: that is your life to love and preserve. You were never a project, you are a person.[14] You are not here to survive a thousand debates.[15] You are here to live your life, right now, as you are. That is your right, that is your power, and that is where we begin. We will talk again soon. For now though, take care of yourself, stay hydrated, eat well, laugh often, and rest well.

Notes and References

Sit and Talk

1 I am pointing out how sometimes people treat me as if I am only a list of separate traits, and not one complete person.

2 I mean that people are not fully understood by looking at just pieces of their identity or experience.

3 I am saying that it is wrong when people talk about someone without including them in the conversation about their own life.

4 I am describing how I kept paying close attention to how some people treat knowledge. Some people are open to learning new things, and others refuse to change what they believe.

5 I am using "dogs of dogma" to describe people who strongly defend harmful beliefs. "Clenched fists" means signs that a person may respond to disagreement with anger, hurtful comments, or controlling behavior.

6 Cresswell, Julia. *Oxford Dictionary of Word Origins*. 3rd ed. Oxford Quick Reference Ser. Oxford: Oxford University Press, Incorporated, 2021.

7 I am asking you to stop and think carefully about this idea. I do not mean to literally chew or roll. Rather I am asking you to pause here to think about the irony of Dogma, which is meant to be a claim to truth or beliefs as unquestionable are actually defined as a perspective. This is also just meant to be an amusing way to compare dogmatic people with dogs, which I do a lot throughout the series, but I don't ever mean it literally.

8 I am using "walking stick" as a symbol for beliefs that help us feel supported. But sometimes beliefs can also be used to control or hurt others. When we are not holding a stick to lean on it then we may be holding a stick that we may use to fight or defend ourselves, which can harm others, especially when they don't have a similar sticks/beliefs. That is a difference in power, an advantage in a conversation that makes the conversation unfair, imbalanced, and that can be abusive.

The S.T.R.A.W.S. Process

1 I am saying that the S.T.R.A.W.S. process is a method you can use again and again to help you deal with dogma. It helps people stay connected, build trust, and take responsibility for their actions in conversations about dogma.

2 "Field of tall straws" is a playful image. I am saying I do not want to overwhelm you with too much information. Instead, I will give you an example from my life to help explain it.

3 I am asking you to think about a made-up picture of the place where I grew up. I use this to help you understand the background and values I come from.

4 I am describing how some people in my community would talk about people from cities in a fearful or suspicious way. I do not mean all hunters think this way.

5 I am explaining that some people wrongly believe that me being a trans woman is not real, but is pretend or fake, like a costume.

6 The image of a child's first attempt to dress is to show that some people see me as clumsy or foolish, which is not true. This assumption is hurtful to me as an adult, but my bigger concern is about how they see me as child-like. Which means that people who think like this tend to see me as someone with less power, less rights, as someone to control or punish. That perspective ignores my maturity, intelligence, and right to be treated as an adult.

7 I am saying that some people do not take me seriously as a real person. They either treat me like a scary story, or like entertainment. Either way, these assumptions tell me that they have made up a story about me and my experiences instead seeking more accurate information.

8 I am saying that each new conversation with a stranger can be unpredictable. "Roll of the dice" means a random encounter and an uncertain outcome. "Walking stick" here is a reference to the earlier example. Which means the person may be bringing strong beliefs that could cause harm in the conversation.

9 I am saying that when I faced danger or unkindness, I used my ability to speak well and think carefully to help me stay safe. This did not always work.

10 I am using the image of making a mask to describe how I tried to hide my true self. I changed how I acted to try to protect myself from harm. I am still healing from the damage this has caused.

11 I am saying that the way I hid my true self did not last. Over time, it broke down and I would eventually remember.

12 I am describing how my true self, the woman I am, was always inside me. Even when I pretended to be someone else, that true voice was strong and protective.

13 I am using "spring" and "harvest" as images to describe how, after years of growth and learning, I was finally ready to share this process with others.

14 I am saying that I feel very happy to be able to write this book and share my ideas. I also want to give thanks to someone else who helped me become the person I am today.

15 I am describing my father dressing up as a scarecrow for Halloween. He was pretending to be a decoration to surprise visitors.

16 I am saying that my father would purposely wait until older kids got close before surprising them in a fun way.

17 I am saying that my father was very open and honest in how he spoke to people. His goal was always to bring people together and find common ground, even if they were very different from each other.

18 I am saying that my father made mistakes sometimes, but he understood that as a parent, his actions would teach me important lessons.

19 I am using "lifeline" and "snorkel" as symbols. I mean that this process helped me survive very difficult times when harmful beliefs (dogma) were overwhelming me.

20 "Endure the suck" is slang for getting through something very unpleasant. "Speak from my roots" means speaking honestly from who I truly am and what I have learned in life.

21 I am saying that even when people tried to silence me, I had been learning, thinking, and writing my ideas in the sides (margins) of my books.

22 I am telling you that this book is not just ideas about a process. Rather, each book in the No More Dogma series is itself a step in the process. Each book also highlights the larger themes from the Bible. Each book also has arguments that some readers may find can useful in their conversations.

23 I am saying that before going deep into details, I will give you a simple summary of the S.T.R.A.W.S. process.

24 I am saying that this book is meant to give you useful skills ("sharp tools") so you can help stand up for people who are not able to speak up for themselves.

To Bark, Bite, and Be

1 I am using the image of a crowbar to say that the S.T.R.A.W.S. process gives you extra strength or help when dealing with hard conversations. It helps you use your life experiences and who you are to handle these talks. I will describe how to use that leverage with a P.R.Y. acronym which I describe in the W.A.G. tool.

2 I am saying that by using this process, you may learn new things about yourself and how you deal with difficult ideas or beliefs (dogma).

3 I am asking you to think about how your past experiences have shaped who you are today. "Witness your becoming" means noticing how you have grown and changed.

4 McAdams, Dan P., Ruthellen Josselson, and Amia Lieblich. Identity and Story: Creating Self in Narrative. The Narrative Study of Lives. (Washington (D.C.): American psychological association, 2006), 16.

5 I am saying that having disagreements in conversations is not a mistake. It is a normal and healthy part of being human.

6 I am saying that when we use this process well, we can stay true to ourselves during hard conversations. We can allow both ourselves and others to change, without forcing anyone or mixing up ideas unfairly.

7 Als, Hilton. "The Revolutionary Writing of bell hooks." The New Yorker, December 16, 2021. https://www.newyorker.com/culture/postscript/the-revolutionary-writing-of-bell-hooks.

8 Hooks, Bell. *Teaching to Transgress: Education as the Practice of Freedom.* (New York London: Routledge, Taylor & Francis Group, 1994), 84.

9 I am saying that I began to question why many Christians accept silence or inaction from God instead of working for justice themselves.

10 I am saying that some Christians avoid helping people now because they believe that justice will only happen in the future by God.

11 I am saying that I chose to actively listen to people who are often ignored or not allowed to speak.

12 LaDuke, Winona. "Masks in the New Millenium" in Recovering the Sacred: The Power of Naming and Claiming. Second Edition. New York, NY: Haymarket Books, 2016.

13 I am saying that most people do not like being forced to speak, being publicly shamed, or being treated as helpless so that someone else can feel like a hero.

14 I am using "group project" as a way to say that I want to work with others to make the world better for everyone.

15 Freire, Paulo, and Donaldo P. Macedo. Pedagogy of the Oppressed: 30th Anniversary Edition. Translated by Myra Bergman Ramos. 30th anniversary edition. (New York: Bloomsbury Publishing, 2014), 53.

16 I am saying that people need to move beyond selfish thinking or pride in order to have better conversations and relationships.

17 Yunkaporta, Tyson. "Lines in the Sand" in Sand Talk: How Indigenous Thinking Can Save the World. Melbourne: Text Publishing, 2019.

18 I am describing a story where Jesus chooses to stay calm and thoughtful instead of reacting with anger. He gives people a chance to reflect.

19 Anderson, Kim, and Maria Campbell. "Centring Resurgence" in Keetsah-nak: Our Missing and Murdered Indigenous Sisters. First edition. Edmonton (Canada): The University of Alberta Press, 2018

20 I am asking whether to teach people to truly live out love and care for others, or to let their faith become empty habit or ritual ("crumbs and a chrome cup" refers to communion taken without meaning).

A Welcome to All Readers

1 I am saying that while this book uses Bible quotes, I do not treat the Bible as the only or ultimate source of truth.

2 I am saying that humor should be used thoughtfully, not to hurt others.

3 I am saying that humor should challenge those in power, not target or harm people who have less power. I will talk about power dynamics throughout the *No More Dogma* series, but for a preview look at the checklist on power in the W.A.G. tool.

4 This is a humorous play on words. I am pointing out that sometimes people judge others about private matters when they should not.

My Un-Apologetic Approach

1 I am using this image to say that sometimes reading the Bible can feel confusing or personal, like reading messages meant for someone else from another time.

2 I am saying that people with rigid harmful beliefs often pick Bible verses and read them in a limited way to try to prove their point, even if that is not what the verse really meant.

I Swear to Tell The Truth

1 I am comparing my use of curse words to a magician's use of sleight of hand. Sleight of hand is a way of controlling your attention to create an illusion. I do something similar with curse words. I use curse words to make you pay more attention to an idea or to create emotional distance from a harmful idea.

The W.A.G. Tool

1 I am using playful language to say that I enjoy having helpful worksheets or tools like this one, and that many people in queer communities do too. I am also making a joke about the W.A.G. tool being like a "spreadsheet" which sounds like separating bed sheets to get into bed.

2 I am saying that this tool is designed to help you be your full self in conversations, not to hide or pretend.

3 I am using playful language comparing this to a dog's body: first you check the situation ("sniff"), then you decide how to respond — kindly, firmly, or by setting a boundary.

4 I am saying that the middle part of the tool helps you remember what matters to you — your values, ideas, and points you want to make.

The Guard at the Gate

1 Gage, Matilda Joslyn. "Woman, Church & State; The Original Exposé of Male Collaboration Against the Female Sex." Accessed November 20, 2023. https://www.gutenberg.org/cache/epub/45580/pg45580-images.html.

2 This is a metaphor. I do not mean anyone literally bent you backward. I mean you may have felt overwhelmed, verbally attacked, or emotionally pushed by people aggressively quoting the Bible in a harmful way.

3 "Canines of convictions" is a metaphor. I am saying that dogma acts like stubborn, unthinking dogs — people holding rigid beliefs that they refuse to examine.

4 This is a common idiom. It means: can people with old, rigid beliefs learn new, better ways of thinking?

5 This is playful imagery. I do not mean literal bacon or dog training. I mean: can we offer kindness or persuasive ideas to encourage dogmatic people to listen?

6 This is a metaphor. I do not mean literally adopting an animal. I mean trying to help someone without fully knowing what they need emotionally or mentally.

7 Again, metaphor. This means approaching a hostile or defensive person with the hope of calming them — but they may react badly.

8 Metaphor. I am saying that even if we offer kindness, sometimes the conversation still turns into a fight (verbal argument), not a peaceful discussion.

9 Simile. I am saying that dogmatic people often react with fear, defensiveness, or aggression when challenged, much like a frightened stray animal.

10 "Bash back" is figurative. I do not mean physical violence. I mean responding strongly and effectively to bigoted ideas.

11 Metaphor. I do not mean literally carving. I mean figuring out which harmful beliefs we need to challenge and remove from the conversation.

12 Metaphor. I am saying that sometimes trying to change someone's thinking feels slow and tangled — like pulling at fishing nets that resist movement.

13 Extended metaphor. I am saying that sometimes asking questions or challenging one small belief can unintentionally cause a person to feel like their whole belief system is falling apart.

14 Figurative language. I mean that when I tried to ask gentle questions, the other person sometimes felt attacked instead.

15 "Woven together" is figurative. I mean that the ideas and tools in this process are connected and designed to work together. This is also an extended metaphor from earlier where I described interacting with fishnets is many different threads being woven together, creating a structure similar to a persons perspective being woven together with various beliefs, ideas, experiences and other sources of knowledge.

16 "Putting down" is figurative. I mean stopping or challenging hateful speech.

17 "Killer knowledge" is slang/hyperbole and humor together. What I mean by "killer" is very powerful or impactful knowledge. However, I also say killer as a humorous observation: God claims that those who eat from the tree of knowledge in the Garden of Eden would die.

18 "Jaw clenching" is figurative for physical tension caused by frustration or stress. "Knows better now" implies learned experience.

19 "Shrugs" is nonverbal communication — can signal indifference, dismissal, or uncertainty.

20 "Swipes" here is casual/slang for grabbing or taking quickly.

21 "Knows that look" is figurative — implies understanding someone's mood based on expression/body language. "Strides" implies confident walking.

22 Figurative for physical expression of frustration or tension.

23 "Means to me" is figurative for personal emotional significance — not literally meaning something measurable.

24 "Rolls his eyes" is nonverbal sarcasm or dismissal.

25 All are figurative bodily responses to emotional stress or anger.

26 "Shakes the fruit" is figurative — not threatening violence, just expressing frustration.

27 Eve is talking about a contrast between prophecy and observed result, challenging a literal interpretation.

28 "Know better" is figurative, meaning a claim to superior knowledge.

29 "Pushes off," "glares," and "closes the distance" are nonverbal cues of confrontation.

30 The imagery of the fleeing fawn and birds is poetic/symbolic, reflecting a rising tension and unease in the scene.

31 "Chest begins to burn" is figurative — describing strong emotional response (anger, sense of justice).

32 "Glares" is nonverbal communication — indicates anger or frustration.

33 "Journey through the wormhole" is a playful sci-fi metaphor — not a literal event.

34 "Clothed in knowledge" is figurative, which means she is prepared with understanding, wisdom, and boundaries.

35 "Anchoring" is figurative — meaning that dogma provides a stable reference point for beliefs, not a literal anchor.

36 "Still water can become intellectually stagnant" is figurative — stagnant water is an image for ideas or beliefs that do not evolve, becoming stale or unhelpful.

37 "Keeps you grounded" is figurative — meaning that dogma provides a sense of security and constancy.

38 "Force group cohesion" is figurative — it means to pressure or compel people to remain united, not literally forcing them.

39 "Discern between your differences" is figurative — it means to understand and evaluate the differences in viewpoints or beliefs.

40 Figurative. It means trying to intervene in a heated argument or conflict using calming or positive methods. "Stretch out" is also figurative. It means to pause and prepare mentally.

41 "Push back" and "digging in our heels" are figurative. It means resisting strongly and standing firm in one's views.

42 "Straw man" is an idiom. It refers to a misrepresented version of someone else's argument that is easier to attack.

43 "Dogmatic against dogma" means using rigid thinking while trying to fight rigid thinking.

How Self-Care Helps Us Look Forward

1 "Converse with ourselves" is figurative. It means thinking deeply or reflecting internally.

2 If your curious to know more, Dr. Kounios and Dr. Beeman are cognitive neuroscientists who wrote a great book about these realizations!

Kounios, John, and Mark Beeman. *The Eureka Factor: Aha Moments, Creative Insight, and the Brain*. First edition. New York: Random House, 2015.

3 Cameron, Julia. *The Artist's Way: A Spiritual Path to Higher Creativity*. 25th anniversary edition. New York, New York: TarcherPeregree, 2016.

4 Lamott, Anne. *Bird by Bird: Some Instructions on Writing and Life*. 1st Anchor Books ed. New York: Anchor Books, 1995.

5 This is a personification: routines of course do not teach, but the repetition of actions leads to learning.

6 "Off" is a common but vague phrase. It means that something about a person's behavior or mood seems unusual or wrong.

7 Hermans, Hubert J. M., and Els Hermans-Jansen. *Self-Narratives: The Construction of Meaning in Psychotherapy*. New York: Guilford Press, 1995.

8 Hubert J. M. Hermans, *Liberation in the Face of Uncertainty: A New Development in Dialogical Self Theory* (Cambridge: Cambridge University Press, 2021), 132.

9 These are examples of colloquial expressions used to resist change or new approaches to care.

10 Haslanger, Sally Anne. *Resisting Reality: Social Construction and Social Critique*. (New York: Oxford University Press, 2012), 184.

11 Lorde, Audre. *A Burst of Light: And Other Essays*. Ixia Press edition. Mineola, New York: Ixia Press, 2017.

12 "Widen the gap" means increasing division or conflict. "Walked through life together" means having shared understanding or connection.

13 Hochschild, Arlie Russell, ed. "I was Invisible to Myself," In *The Outsourced Self: What Happens When We Pay Others to Live Our Lives for Us*. 1. Picador ed. New York: Picador, 2013.

14 "People pleaser" and "savior complex" are colloquial terms for someone who prioritizes others' needs excessively, sometimes to their own detriment.

15 This is a form of wordplay. It means that mis-prioritizing self-care can lead to personal problems.

16 This is an implied meaning. What I refer to here is the experience of struggling with complex tasks when not yet fully alert.

Boundaries for Being

1 Idiom. It means LGBTQIA+ people are not just interested in this issue—they are personally involved and affected.

2 Implied meaning. It suggests that wearing clothes is a human trait and a way to express personhood and boundaries.

3 Colloquial phrase. It means you are not as clever or sneaky as you think.

4 "The birds and the bees" is an idiom for sex education. The sentence also plays on the phrase with a humorous literal reference to an environmental issue that is important to me. Here is one of my favorite books about bees:

Wilson, Joseph S., and Messinger Carril, Olivia. *The Bees in Your Backyard: A Guide to North America's Bees*. Princeton, NJ: Princeton University Press, 2015.

5 Granted, not every trans woman experiences bottom dysphoria.

6 Tawwab, Nedra Glover. *Set Boundaries, Find Peace: A Guide to Reclaiming Yourself*. New York: TarcherPerigee, 2021.

7 Figurative. It means experiencing sudden discomfort or anxiety.

8 The "male gaze" is a feminist theory term. Refers to objectifying looks from men toward women.

9 To "clutch their pearls" is an older idiom. It means people with enough wealth for jewelry who will act shocked or offended, often in an exaggerated or performative way.

10 "Tend to go feral" is colloquial and figurative. It means becoming very angry or defensive.

11 "Want access" is figurative. It means a desire to intrude on my privacy or personal life.

12 Stryker, Susan. *Transgender History: The Roots of Today's Revolution*. Second edition, Revised edition. Berkeley: Seal Press, 2017.

13 Gill-Peterson, Julian. *Histories of the Transgender Child*. Minneapolis: University of Minnesota Press, 2018.

14 Heyam, Kit. *Before We Were Trans: A New History of Gender*. First Trade Paperback Edition. New York: Seal Press, 2024.

I am Loved, I am Known

1 "Our authority can be our authenticity" is figurative. It means your personal truth and identity give you credibility.

2 A "conversing community" is an abstract phrase. It means communicating what other needs still require attention within a supportive community.

3 Although I am critical of Brene Brown here, I am still a fan of her work. Brown's *Atlas of the Heart* is especially important for those who want to understand emotions better.

Brown, Brené. *Braving the Wilderness: The Quest for True Belonging and the Courage to Stand Alone*. First edition. New York: Random House, 2017.

4 Sara Ahmed wrote an incredible book about how complaints to the powerful have mutated organizations and communities into entities that handle complaints rather than address complaints. Ahmed, Sara. *Complaint!* Durham London: Duke University Press, 2021. https://doi.org/10.1515/9781478022336.

5 McIntosh, Colin and Cambridge University Press, eds. *Cambridge Advanced Learner's Dictionary*. Fourth edition. (Cambridge: Cambridge University Press, 2013), 782.

6 McIntosh, Colin and Cambridge University Press, eds. *Cambridge Advanced Learner's Dictionary*. Fourth edition. (Cambridge: Cambridge University Press, 2013), 92.

7 "Harbor" is figurative. Here it means to contain and protect. What is being "harbored" here are "Bible bashing" verses from the Bible. This colloquial could also be an idiom, although it is almost literal as it does mean using the Bible to attack or criticize others. However, the attack is not physical, rather it is an aggressive and judgmental communication.

8 "Buried behind a dug in dogmatic" is both figurative and alliteration. It means hidden by stubborn beliefs.

Considering Perspectives

1 "Judged an outfit on the rack" is a metaphor. It compares judging self-care too quickly to judging clothing in a store without trying it on.

2 "An outfit made of inferior materials and is now showing signs of wear" is figurative. It refers to outdated or worn-out personal habits or self-concepts.

3 Turner, Jonathan H. Theoretical Sociology: A Concise Introduction to Twelve Sociological Theories. (Los Angeles: SAGE Publications, 2014), 100.

4 Turner, Jonathan H. Theoretical Sociology: A Concise Introduction to Twelve Sociological Theories. (Los Angeles: SAGE Publications, 2014), 102.

5 This is metaphorical. It means to reveal or expose personal details about one's sexuality, similar to the ideal of "coming out", which is also a personal choice.

6 Hatch, Mary Jo, and Majken Schultz, eds. Organizational Identity: A Reader. Repr. Oxford Management Readers. (Oxford: Oxford Univ. Press, 2010), 56.

Integrity, Intent, and Impact

[1] "Have a way of" is an idiom. It means funerals often result in arguments.

[2] "Ultimate no" is metaphorical. It means death is a final, undeniable fact.

[3] This is a simile. It compares the emotional experience of a funeral to observing changing seasons.

[4] This is a simile. It compares the feeling of loss to a black hole with strong pull and emotional weight.

[5] "Attracts a gathering" and "raw and rare relating" are abstract. It means death brings people together in an emotionally open way.

[6] "Ground us in reality" is a metaphor. It means helping people stay focused and clear-headed.

[7] This is metaphorical. It means when it is time to engage in a conversation.

[8] This is figurative. It means he made himself the focus of the conversation.

[9] "Tiny red flag" is a metaphor. It means a small warning sign.

[10] Siegel, Daniel J., and Tina Payne Bryson. *The Whole-Brain Child: 12 Revolutionary Strategies to Nurture Your Child's Developing Mind*. New York: Delacorte Press, 2011.

Self-Care, Not Self Centered

[1] If you would like some historic examples then look up the history of the King James Bible. If you are curious about some deeper reading look at Fulton, Thomas. *The Book of Books: Biblical Interpretation, Literary Culture, and the Political Imagination from Erasmus to Milton*. Philadelphia: University of Pennsylvania Press, 2021.

[2] There are many great studies about this phenomenon, but for the sake of exemplifying my own ironic egotism I will offer my favorite: Geyser-Fouche, Ananda, and Carli Fourie. "Inclusivity in the Old Testament." *HTS Teologiese Studies / Theological Studies* 73, no. 4 (April 21, 2017): 9 pages. https://doi.org/10.4102/hts.v73i4.4761.

[3] Dr. Roland Cox provides a wonderful study about the cultural bias in biblical interpretation.

Cox, Roland. "Cultural Biases in New Testament Interpretation: Explaining Them Using Hofstede's Cultural Dimensions," 2018. https://doi.org/10.13140/RG.2.2.13217.15204.

[4] Here is a great study that covers several biases that connect with a confirmation bias. Chalmers, Aaron. "The Influence of Cognitive Biases on Biblical Interpretation." *Bulletin for Biblical Research* 26, no. 4 (January 1, 2016): 467–80. https://doi.org/10.2307/26371525.

[5] For those of you who enjoy a deep dive into the cognitive science behind religious beliefs, I recommend: *Language, Cognition, and Biblical Exegesis: In-*

terpreting Minds. Paperback edition. London; New York; Oxford; New Delhi; Sydney: Bloomsbury Academic, 2021.

[6] If you want a good book that does not shy away from the full humanity of Jesus, while also criticizing popular faith approaches, then I recommend: Evers-Hood, Ken. *Irrational Jesus: Leading the Fully Human Church*. Eugene, Oregon: Cascade Books, 2016.

[7] If you are curious to see how the Bible was read with a narcissistic bias to support the horrors of the African Apartheid then take a look at: Lombaard, Christo. "Does Contextual Exegesis Require an Affirming Bible? Lessons from 'Apartheid' and 'Africa' as Narcissistic Hermeneutical Keys." *Scriptura: Journal for Contextual Hermeneutics in Southern Africa* 101, no. 1 (January 2009): 274–87. https://doi.org/10.10520/EJC100490.

[8] "Digging in" and "carve out" are metaphors. They mean becoming stubborn and forcing an argument from a self-created and self-centered position.

[9] "Avoid jumping" is literal in the earlier story, but then jumping to conclusions" is used here metaphorically. It means making decisions too quickly.

[10] "Jump in the bed with dogma" is a metaphor. It means accepting dogma too readily or without caution.

[11] When I say "whole grain snacks" here I am making a literal observation as a joke. What they were eating was quite literally unprocessed whole grains.

[12] "Make it rain snacks" is both a playful metaphor and a callback joke. As a metaphor it means miraculously providing food, which God is claimed to have literally done by providing manna from heaven.

[13] "Stretch authority" is a metaphor. It means trying to expand influence.

Love > Bias, Burnout, or Bigotry

[1] "Navigate the give and take" is metaphorical. It means manage the flow and exchanges in a conversation.

[2] I was often prone to burnout as a Pastor and now again as a writer. As I studied burnout I came across a fascinating and thorough text that discusses burnout among healthcare professionals who treat HIV/AIDS in the UK: Miller, David. *Dying to Care: Work, Stress and Burnout in HIV/AIDS Professionals*. 1st ed. Routledge, 2005. https://doi.org/10.4324/9780203982686.

[3] For anyone who wants more information here, which should be all of us, I strongly recommend: Leary, Joy DeGruy, and Randall Robinson. *Post Traumatic Slave Syndrome: America's Legacy of Enduring Injury and Healing*. Chambersburg, PA: Ligtning Source LLC, 2017.

[4] "Possessed as an object to having possessions as a subject" is metaphorical. It contrasts being treated as property with being a person who owns property.

[5] For an in depth look at the moment by moment lives of the formerly enslaved, please consider the Pulitzer Prize Winner Douglas Blackmon's book *Slavery by Another Name*. Blackmon provides a powerful exegetical lens through which to view black lives after the emancipation proclamation. Please go read: Blackmon, Douglas A. *Slavery by Another Name: The Re-Enslavement of Black Americans from the Civil War to World War II*. 1st Anchor Books ed. New York: Anchor Books, 2009.

[6] *We will Shoot Back* is an award winning account of black Mississippians who were compelled to take up arms, and then navigate challenging social situations after. An insightful and vital part of history. Please go read: Umoja, Akinyele Omowale. *We Will Shoot Back: Armed Resistance in the Mississippi Freedom Movement*. New York (N.Y.): New York University Press, 2013.

[7] The New York Times best selling author Henry Louis Gates addresses the historic tension between adapting to survive or resisting a culture heading for Jim Crow laws. I recommend you read this one slowly so you can look up the churches, leaders, and communities mentioned within: Gates, Henry Louis. *Stony the Road: Reconstruction, White Supremacy, and the Rise of Jim Crow*. New York: Penguin Books, 2020.

[8] Of my top 100 favorite books, this is in the top 30. Get a copy now, and pick up an extra copy to gift to your conversation partner: Bloom, Joshua, and Waldo E. Martin. *Black against Empire: The History and Politics of the Black Panther Party*. Berkeley, CA: University of California Press, 2016. https://doi.org/10.1525/9780520966451.

[9] Scholz, Susanne. *Sacred Witness: Rape in the Hebrew Bible*. (Minneapolis, MN: Fortress Press, 2010), 133.

[10] Breiner, Sander J. *Slaughter of the Innocents: Child Abuse through the Ages and Today*. (New York: Plenum Press, 1990), 6.

[11] Swanson, James. *Dictionary of Biblical Languages with Semantic Domains : Hebrew (Old Testament)*. Oak Harbor: Logos Research Systems, Inc., 1997.

[12] This is an accessible resource that you can direct your conversation partner toward as they may already have access to it: Roggio, Sharon "Rocky," dir. *1946: The Mistranslation That Shifted Culture*. Hindsight Productions, 2023. Streaming video. Amazon Prime Video. https://www.amazon.com/1946-Mistranslation-That-Shifted-Culture/dp/B0D6DW5C91.

[13] I've already offered some trigger warnings before, and I want to warn you again here before you read: King, Wilma. *Stolen Childhood: Slave Youth in Nineteenth-Century America*. Bloomington: Indiana University Press, 1995.

The Social Impact of Self-Care

[1] "Tailgaters" and "following so closely" are metaphors. It humorously compares dogmatic followers to cars driving too close, which make collisions, and conversations with conflict more common.

[2] "Back off your bumper" is metaphorical. It means give space or stop being overbearing.

Return to the Heart

[1] Note: "Distorts," "flattens your story," "attacks your humanity," "language designed to erase you" are metaphors. These phrases describe how dogma misrepresents and harms people.

[2] "Seeking erasure" is metaphorical. It means trying to invalidate or erase someone's identity.

[3] "Staying human" is abstract. It means maintaining your full sense of self.

[4] "Brittle, performative version" is metaphorical. It means an emotionally fragile, inauthentic version shaped by external pressures.

[5] "Softness," "sharp," "silent," "shamed" are metaphorical. They describe emotional states and behaviors encouraged or discouraged by society.

[6] "Stay vivid" and "render in grayscale" are metaphors. They describe maintaining vibrancy and individuality against efforts to dull or erase it.

[7] "Retreat from justice" and "return to wholeness" are metaphors. They describe self-care as a way to maintain personal integrity, not avoidance.

[8] "Compression," "cut away at your whole being" are metaphors. They describe being pressured to diminish yourself.

[9] "Atmosphere taught" and "fullness was unsafe" are metaphors. They describe how an environment can make authenticity feel dangerous.

[10] "Wants less," "segments," "bent out of shape" are metaphors. They describe being reduced or distorted. "Mold" is metaphorical. It refers to a rigid framework or expectation that is forced upon you.

[11] "Walk away" can be literal or figurative here. It means to leave or disengage. "Hold your name" is metaphorical. It means respect your identity. "Arms to hold all of you" is literal and metaphorical here. It means acceptance and support for your whole self.

[12] "Cut out pieces of yourself" is metaphorical. It means deny or hide parts of your identity.

[13] "Recover your voice" is metaphorical here. It means regain your ability to speak up or express yourself. "Hearing your own heartbeat" is metaphorical here but it can also be literal. It means being attuned to your own life and vitality.

[14] "Project" is metaphorical here. It means an object to be fixed or improved upon.

[15] "Survive a thousand debates" is figurative. It means you are not here to endlessly justify your existence.